Contents

The Scientific Process

'How Science Works' is all about the scientific process — how we develop and test scientific ideas.
It's what scientists do all day, every day (well, except at coffee time — never come between a scientist and their coffee).

Scientists Come Up with **Theories** — Then **Test Them**...

Science tries to explain **how** and **why** things happen — it **answers questions**. It's all about seeking and gaining **knowledge** about the world around us. Scientists do this by **asking** questions and **suggesting** answers and then **testing** them, to see if they're correct — this is the **scientific process**.

1) **Ask** a question — make an **observation** and ask **why or how** it happens.
   E.g. why is trypsin (an enzyme) found in the small intestine but not in the stomach?

2) **Suggest** an answer, or part of an answer, by forming a **theory** (a possible **explanation** of the observations) e.g. pH affects the activity of enzymes. (Scientists also sometimes form a **model** too — a **simplified picture** of what's physically going on.)

3) Make a **prediction** or **hypothesis** — a **specific testable statement**, based on the theory, about what will happen in a test situation. E.g. trypsin will be active at pH 8 (the pH of the small intestine) but inactive at pH 2 (the pH of the stomach).

4) Carry out a **test** — to provide **evidence** that will support the prediction (or help to disprove it). E.g. measure the rate of reaction of trypsin at various pH levels.

The evidence supported Quentin's Theory of Flammable Burps.

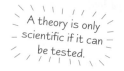

A theory is only scientific if it can be tested.

...Then They **Tell** Everyone About Their **Results**...

The results are **published** — scientists need to let others know about their work. Scientists publish their results in **scientific journals**. These are just like normal magazines, only they contain **scientific reports** (called papers) instead of the latest celebrity gossip.

1) Scientific reports are similar to the **lab write-ups** you do in school. And just as a lab write-up is **reviewed** (marked) by your teacher, reports in scientific journals undergo **peer review** before they're published.

2) The report is sent out to **peers** — other scientists who are experts in the **same area**. They examine the data and results, and if they think that the conclusion is reasonable it's **published**. This makes sure that work published in scientific journals is of a **good standard**.

3) But peer review **can't guarantee** the science is **correct** — other scientists still need to **reproduce** it.

4) Sometimes **mistakes** are made and flawed work is published. Peer review **isn't perfect** but it's probably the best way for scientists to self-regulate their work and to publish **quality reports**.

...Then **Other Scientists** Will **Test** the Theory Too

Other scientists read the published theories and results, and try to **test the theory** themselves. This involves:
- Repeating the **exact same experiments**.
- Using the theory to make **new predictions** and then testing them with **new experiments**.

If the **Evidence** Supports a Theory, It's **Accepted** — for Now

1) If all the experiments in all the world provide good evidence to back it up, the theory is thought of as **scientific 'fact'** (for now).

2) But it will never become **totally indisputable** fact. Scientific **breakthroughs or advances** could provide new ways to question and test the theory, which could lead to **new evidence** that **conflicts** with the current evidence. Then the testing starts all over again...

And this, my friend, is the **tentative nature of scientific knowledge** — it's always **changing** and **evolving**.

AS-Level

man

ogy

...ricky — no question about that.
... revise properly and practise hard.

...s on all the theory you need,
...estions... lots of them.
...-up and exam-style questions.

...the whole thing vaguely entertaining for you.

Complete Revision and Practice
Exam Board: AQA

Editors:
Ellen Bowness, Charlotte Burrows, Thomas Cain, Katherine Craig, Andy Park, Jane Towle.

Contributors:
Gloria Barnett, James Foster, Barbara Green, Liz Masters, Stephen Phillips, Adrian Schmit, Sophie Watkins, Anna-fe Williamson.

Proofreaders:
Glenn Rogers, Sue Hocking.

Published by CGP

ISBN: 978 1 84762 119 1

With thanks to Jan Greenway for the copyright research.

Graph on page 6 copyright © 2001 Massachusetts Medical Society. All rights reserved.

Graph on page 7 from Hamajima, N. Hirose, K. Tajima, K. et al. Alcohol, tobacco and breast cancer - collaborative reanalysis of individual data from 53 epidemiological studies, including 58,515 women with breast cancer and 95,067 women without the disease. BJC 2002; 87:1234-45.

Data used to construct the graphs on page 28 and page 29 from National Statistics online. Reproduced under the terms of the Click-Use licence.

MMR graph on page 35 adapted from H. Honda, Y. Shimizu, M. Rutter. No effect of MMR withdrawal on the incidence of autism: a total population study. Journal of Child Psychology and Psychiatry 2005; 46(6):572-579.

Data used to construct the Hib graph on page 35 reproduced with kind permission from the Health Protection Agency.

Data used to construct the graph on page 45 from R. Doll, R. Peto, J. Boreham, I Sutherland. Mortality in relation to smoking: 50 years' observations on male British doctors. BMJ 2004; 328:1519.

With thanks to Cancer Research UK for permission to reproduce the graphs on page 55. Cancer Research UK, http://info.cancerresearchuk.org/cancerstats/types/lung/mortality/, January 2008. Cancer Research UK, http://info.cancerresearchuk.org/cancerstats/types/lung/smoking/, January 2008.

Data used to construct the table on page 55 from E. Cho, B. A. Rosner, D. Feskanich, G. A. Colditz. Risk Factors and Individual Probabilities of Melanoma for Whites. Journal of Clinical Oncology 2005; 23(12): 2669-2675.

With thanks to Science Photo Library for permission to reproduce the photographs used on pages 51 and 77.

Groovy website: www.cgpbooks.co.uk
Jolly bits of clipart from CorelDRAW®
Printed by Elanders Ltd, Newcastle upon Tyne.

The Scientific Process

So scientists need evidence to back up their theories. They get it by carrying out experiments, and when that's not possible they carry out studies. But why bother with science at all? We want to know as much as possible so we can use it to try and improve our lives (and because we're nosy).

Evidence Comes from Lab Experiments...

1) Results from **controlled experiments** in **laboratories** are **great**.

2) A lab is the easiest place to **control variables** so that they're all **kept constant** (except for the one you're investigating).

3) This means you can draw meaningful **conclusions**.

For example, if you're investigating how temperature affects the rate of an enzyme-controlled reaction you need to keep everything but the temperature constant, e.g. the pH of the solution, the concentration of the solution etc.

...and Well-Designed Studies

1) There are things you **can't** investigate in a lab, e.g. whether stress causes heart attacks. You have to do a study instead.

2) You still need to try and make the study as controlled as possible to make it **more reliable**. But in reality it's **very hard** to control **all the variables** that **might** be having an effect.

3) You can do things to help, e.g. have **matched groups** — **choose two groups** of people (those who have quite stressful jobs and those who don't) who are **as similar as possible** (same mix of ages, same mix of diets etc.). But you can't easily rule out every possibility.

Samantha thought her study was very well designed — especially the fitted bookshelf.

See pages 82-84 for more on study design.

Society Makes Decisions Based on Scientific Evidence

1) Lots of scientific work eventually leads to **important discoveries** or breakthroughs that could **benefit humankind**.

2) These results are **used by society** (that's you, me and everyone else) to **make decisions** — about the way we live, what we eat, what we drive, etc.

3) All sections of society use scientific evidence to make decisions, e.g. politicians use it to devise policies and individuals use science to make decisions about their own lives.

Other factors can **influence** decisions about science or the way science is used:

Economic factors

- Society has to consider the **cost** of implementing changes based on scientific conclusions — e.g. the **NHS** can't afford the most expensive drugs without **sacrificing** something else.

- Scientific research is **expensive** so companies won't always develop new ideas — e.g. developing new drugs is costly, so pharmaceutical companies often only invest in drugs that are likely to make them **money**.

Social factors

- **Decisions** affect **people's lives** — E.g. scientists may suggest **banning smoking** and **alcohol** to prevent health problems, but shouldn't **we** be able to **choose** whether **we** want to smoke and drink or not?

Environmental factors

- Scientists believe **unexplored regions** like remote parts of rainforests might contain **untapped drug** resources. But some people think we shouldn't **exploit** these regions because any interesting finds may lead to **deforestation** and **reduced biodiversity** in these areas.

So there you have it — how science works...

Hopefully these pages have given you a nice intro to how science works, e.g. what scientists do to provide you with 'facts'. You need to understand this, as you're expected to know how science works — for the exam and for life.

Balanced Diet

I don't know about you, but I can't think of a better way to kick off a Biology book than with a whistle-stop tour of diet. Eat properly and you'll be a better person, plus it'll help you concentrate more and work harder...

A **Balanced Diet** Supplies All the **Essential Nutrients**

A balanced diet gives you all the **nutrients** you need, plus **fibre** and **water**. There are **five** important nutrients — **carbohydrates**, **proteins**, **fats**, **vitamins** and **mineral salts**. Each nutrient has different functions in the body:

NUTRIENTS	FUNCTIONS
Carbohydrates	Provide energy.
Fats (lipids)	Act as an energy store, provide insulation, make up cell membranes, physically protect organs.
Proteins	Needed for growth, the repair of tissues and to make enzymes.
Vitamins	Different vitamins have different functions, e.g. vitamin D is needed for calcium absorption, vitamin K is needed for blood clotting.
Mineral salts	Different mineral salts have different functions, e.g. iron is needed to make haemoglobin in the blood, calcium is needed for bone formation.

Mmm... paper plates, delicious and nutritious...

Fibre	Aids movement of food through gut.
Water	It is used in chemical reactions. We need a constant supply to replace water lost through urinating, breathing and sweating.

A **Healthy Diet** Should be **High** in **Fruit** and **Veg** and **Low** in **Salt** and **Fat**

Current **advice** from the **World Health Organisation** and the **Department of Health** is that we should eat a diet **high in fruit and vegetables** and **low in salt and fat**. This advice is based on **scientific studies**, which have shown that this type of diet can **lower blood pressure** and **reduce** the chances of suffering from conditions like **heart disease**, **stroke** and **cancer**.

We're advised to eat **plenty of fruits and vegetables** (at least five portions a day) because:

1) They're a good source of **vitamins**, **minerals** and **fibre** — which are all **essential** in a healthy diet.

2) Filling up on fruits and vegetables (instead of fatty foods) can help you maintain a **healthy weight**.

3) Studies have shown that eating plenty of fruits and vegetables can **reduce the risk** of **heart disease** and some types of **cancer**.

We're advised to eat **less salt and fat** because:

1) Reducing salt intake has been shown to **lower blood pressure** and **reduce** the risk of **heart disease** and **stroke**.

2) Fat has a **high energy content**. You can put on **weight** if you eat **too much** without doing enough **exercise** — this can result in other health problems, like **obesity**.

3) Eating too much **saturated fat** can increase the amount of **cholesterol** in the blood, which **increases the risk of heart disease** (see p. 44).

Adults are recommended to eat no more than **6 g** of salt per day. This is because several **studies** have shown a strong **link** between **high salt intake** and **high blood pressure**. Before this recommendation was made, the evidence linking salt intake to blood pressure was **reviewed** by an **expert committee** to check its **validity**.

Balanced Diet

Foods can be Ranked using GI and GL

GI and GL can be used to help people decide what types of food to eat.

GI (GLYCAEMIC INDEX)

GI is a measure of how **quickly** the **carbohydrates** in different foods raise our blood sugar level after eating.

1) The carbohydrates in foods with a **high GI** (e.g. sweets, white bread) break down and are absorbed **quickly** — our blood glucose level rises **rapidly** after eating.
2) The carbohydrates in foods with a **low GI** (e.g. porridge, wholemeal bread) break down and are absorbed **slowly** — our blood glucose level rises **gradually**.
3) To work out the GI of a food, an amount of the food containing **50 g of carbohydrate** is tested.
4) Foods are given a GI value between **0** and **100** — glucose has a GI value of 100.
5) **Endurance athletes** often eat foods with a low GI **before** a competition, to give them **energy** throughout the competition. They then eat foods with a high GI **afterwards** to give them a **quick energy boost**.

> **Isotonic sports drinks** are designed to quickly **replace** glucose, electrolytes and water used up during exercise. Drinks that are isotonic contain the **same concentration** of **solutes** as the body's fluids — helping absorption. Isotonic sports drinks have a **high GI** — the **glucose** they contain doesn't need to be **digested**, so it's **absorbed quickly**.

GL (GLYCAEMIC LOAD)

GL is calculated from **GI**. It takes into account the **amount of carbohydrate** in an **average portion** of food.

1) For example, the GI for a watermelon is **high**, but you'd have to eat a **whole watermelon** to get 50 g of carbohydrate (used to work out the GI).
2) In reality, you'd only eat a piece of watermelon, containing a lot **less** than 50 g of carbohydrate — so watermelon has a **low GL**. GL is a more useful measurement for the amount of food people actually eat.

Gut Bacteria Aid Digestion

Gut bacteria are bacteria that **live** in the **digestive system**. They're found in **large numbers** in the **colon**.
Gut bacteria have several useful functions.

1) They help the body **break down** some types of **indigestable** carbohydrates, releasing extra **nutrients** for use by the body.
2) They **prevent** the growth of **harmful** bacteria by **competing** with them for food and space.
3) Some gut species (e.g. *Escherichia coli*) **produce Vitamin K**, adding to the amount we get from our diet. Vitamin K has an important role in blood clotting.

Practice Questions

Q1 Why do athletes eat foods with a low GI before an event?
Q2 Why might someone find the glycaemic load more useful than glycaemic index?
Q3 Describe the role of gut bacteria.

Exam Question

Q1 A dietician is giving a patient advice about eating a healthy diet.

a) The patient is told that a healthy diet should include carbohydrates, fats, protein, fibre and water. Suggest one role for each of these nutrients. [5 marks]

b) Why are we advised to eat a diet high in fruits and vegetables but low in salt and fat? [4 marks]

Gin — my favourite ice 'n' tonic drink...

Without all those bacteria in our gut we'd be snookered — they have loads of important roles. There are over 400 different species of bacteria in our colon and bacteria make up about 60 percent of all our poo — bet you didn't know that.

Diet and Disease

Eat too much of the wrong foods and you could end up with health problems. Scientists are always carrying out studies to find links between diet and disease. So, before you tuck into that deep-fried chocolate bar, read on...

Obesity and Type 2 Diabetes are Linked to Unhealthy Diets

A lot of **processed** foods, like ready meals and fast food, are often **high** in **salt** and **fat**. They tend to have **lower vitamin** and **mineral** content than fresh food. Consumption of processed food has **increased** loads over recent years. This, combined with a decrease in **physical activity**, has been linked to an increase in conditions like **obesity** and **type 2 diabetes**.

OBESITY

1) **Obesity** is a common medical condition.
2) People gain body weight when they eat more calories than they work off.
3) People are said to be obese if they have a **body mass index** (BMI) of **over 30** and so much body fat that it causes **health problems**.
4) Obesity can **increase** the risk of **diseases**, such as heart disease, and **lowers** life expectancy.

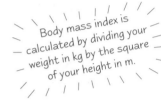
Body mass index is calculated by dividing your weight in kg by the square of your height in m.

DIABETES

1) **Diabetes** is a condition where the body **can't regulate** the amount of **glucose** in the **blood** properly.
2) This is usually because of a lack of the hormone **insulin** — the hormone that regulates our blood glucose level. There are two types of diabetes.
3) In **type 1** diabetes the body can't produce enough insulin.
4) In **type 2** diabetes the insulin that's produced **doesn't work well** — cells become **resistant to insulin**.
5) Too much body fat can cause cells to become insulin resistant, so in most cases type 2 diabetes is linked to **obesity**.

You Might Have to Evaluate Some Data About Diet and Disease

In the exam you could be given some data and asked to evaluate the strength of a **link** between **diet** and **disease**. So here's one we prepared earlier:

EXAMPLE

In 2001 a study was carried out on **412** American adults, to investigate the link between **diet** and **blood pressure**. Participants were screened to make sure that people who drank a large amount of **alcohol** and those on certain **medications** weren't included.

Each participant was randomly allocated one of **two diets** to follow. The first diet was based on a **typical American diet**. The second diet was a **low-fat diet**, high in fresh fruit, vegetables and low-fat dairy foods, and low in total fat and saturated fat. All participants ate foods with **high**, **medium** and **low** sodium (salt) content for **30 days** at a time. After each 30-day period their blood pressure was recorded. The participants were supplied with all of their food throughout the study. The study was **published** in the **New England Journal of Medicine**. The graph opposite shows the results of this study.

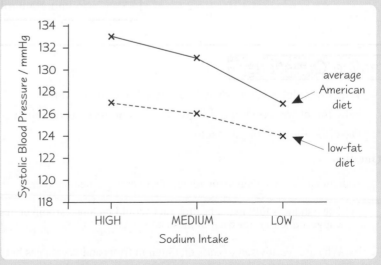

Diet and Disease

You might be asked to:

1) **Describe the data** — The graph shows a **positive correlation** between a **high-fat diet** and **high blood pressure**. It also shows a positive correlation between a **high-salt diet** and **high blood pressure**.

See pages 82-84 for more about interpreting data.

2) **Draw conclusions** — The fact that there's a correlation doesn't mean that a high-fat or high-salt diet **causes** high blood pressure — there may be **other factors** involved. For example, some people might have decreased their level of exercise during the study and this could have caused the increase in blood pressure. Some of these factors were **controlled** in the study to make the results more reliable — people who drank a lot of alcohol and those on certain medications were excluded as these can both affect blood pressure. So the only conclusion that you can draw is that there's a **link** between dietary fat intake and blood pressure (and a link between dietary salt intake and blood pressure).

3) **Evaluate the methodology** — you'll need to think about things like **sample size** and **how long** the study was carried out for.

The larger the sample size the more reliable the results.

- In this study 412 people were tested. This is a fairly **large sample size** so it gives a good **indication** of the **link** between diet and blood pressure. But you have to be careful when **applying** the conclusions of a study to a **whole population**. In this case, the American population is around 300 million people — 412 suddenly feels like a small sample size.

- The **period of time** over which this study was carried out was **quite short**. Participants were only on the high- or low-fat diet for **three months** in total, and on the high, medium or low sodium diets for only **30 days** at a time. This makes it difficult to draw accurate conclusions about the **long-term** effects of a high-fat or high-salt diet on blood pressure, but conclusions about **short-term** effects can be drawn.

- The participants were **supplied** with all their **food** throughout the study, which increases the reliability of the results. But some people might have snacked between meals and could have been **untruthful** about what they had eaten, which would decrease the reliability.

Practice Questions

Q1 Explain why many processed foods could be considered unhealthy.

Q2 What is obesity?

Q3 What is diabetes?

Exam Question

Q1 The graph opposite shows the results from a study into the link between breast cancer and alcohol consumption. The study used data about 58 515 women with breast cancer and 95 067 women without.

Estimated cumulative incidence of breast cancer per 100 women in developed countries, according to the number of alcoholic drinks consumed each day

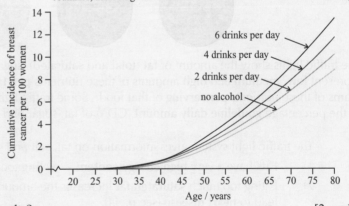

a) What conclusions can be drawn from these results? [2 marks]

b) One student writes the following statement: 'There is a correlation between breast cancer and alcohol consumption, so alcohol causes cancer.' Is he correct? Explain your answer. [2 marks]

c) The study appeared in the British Journal of Cancer and was peer-reviewed before being published. Explain what peer review is. [1 mark]

The chocolate diet — the only one I can actually stick to...

You may wonder why you have to do all this stuff about data. Well, apart from it being really, really interesting, the conclusions that scientists make from studies like this can affect our everyday lives. This study of salt and blood pressure provided part of the data used to lower the recommended intake of salt for adults from 9 g to no more than 6 g per day.

Evaluating the Nutritional Value of Food

Eyes bigger than your belly? Bitten off more than you can chew? Time to learn about the nutritional value of food...

Food Labels Provide Nutritional Information

Most food labels show nutritional information in a **table**.
Have a look at this label taken from some lasagne:

	Per 100 g	Per portion (550 g)
Energy	517 kJ 124 kcal	2843 kJ 682 kcal
Protein	6.0 g	33.0 g
Carbohydrate (of which sugars)	9.0 g 0.2 g	49.5 g 1.1 g
Fat (of which saturates)	5.0 g 2.0 g	27.5 g 11.0 g
Fibre	3.8 g	20.9 g
Sodium	0.1 g	0.6 g
Salt equivalent	0.3 g	1.7 g

Nutritional information is usually given for 100 g of product and for one serving.

Energy is measured in kilojoules (kJ) or Calories (kcal).

Both total carbohydrate (long chains of sugar molecules) and total sugar (simple sugar molecules) are usually shown.

Both total fat and total saturated fat are usually shown. Too much saturated fat is bad for you (see below).

Sodium or salt or both may be shown.

The amount of each nutrient is given in grams (g).

Despite having 2 grams of fat per portion, Margaret was going to eat every single one.

Traffic Light Labels Give Quick Nutritional Information

In addition to food tables, nutritional information can also be presented using the **traffic light** system. This system was devised to help consumers spot **healthier foods** at a **glance**. Have a look at this traffic light label, which shows the same information as the table above:

HIGH Fat 27.5 g   HIGH Saturates 11.0 g   LOW Sugar 1.1 g   MEDIUM Salt 1.7 g

The traffic lights show the amount of **fat** (total and saturated), **sugar** and **salt** in food. The **green**, **orange** and **red** colours represent **low**, **medium** and **high** amounts of these nutrients **per 100 g** of a food. The numbers show the number of **grams** of these nutrients **per serving** of that food. Some traffic light labels also show the number of **Calories** per serving, or the percentage **guideline daily amount** (GDA) of fat, sugar and salt that the food provides.

The traffic light system gives information on fat, salt and sugar because:

1) **Fats** have a very **high energy content** — eating too much may lead to problems like **obesity**.

2) Eating too much **saturated fat** increases the amount of **cholesterol** in our blood, which can lead to **heart disease** (see p. 44).

3) Eating too much **sugar** can cause **weight gain**.

4) Eating too much **salt** can increase **blood pressure**, which is a risk factor for **heart disease**.

Other Information may be Present on Food Packets

The packaging will tell the consumer if the food contains any common **allergens** (e.g. chemicals in nuts), which is handy if they have a **food allergy**. There will also be a '**use by**' or '**best before**' date. Some packets say whether the food is **organic** or **fairtrade certified**.

Evaluating the Nutritional Value of Food

You May be Asked to **Evaluate** Nutritional Information

In an exam you may be given two food labels and asked to **comment** on or **compare** their **nutritional value**. Here are two food labels from prepackaged sandwiches.

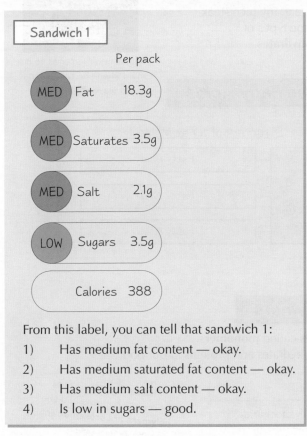

Sandwich 1

Per pack

MED Fat 18.3g

MED Saturates 3.5g

MED Salt 2.1g

LOW Sugars 3.5g

Calories 388

From this label, you can tell that sandwich 1:
1) Has medium fat content — okay.
2) Has medium saturated fat content — okay.
3) Has medium salt content — okay.
4) Is low in sugars — good.

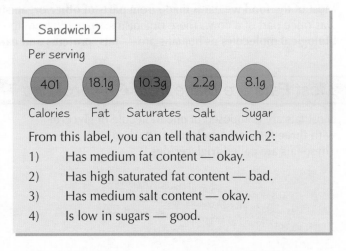

Sandwich 2

Per serving

| 401 | 18.1g | 10.3g | 2.2g | 8.1g |
| Calories | Fat | Saturates | Salt | Sugar |

From this label, you can tell that sandwich 2:
1) Has medium fat content — okay.
2) Has high saturated fat content — bad.
3) Has medium salt content — okay.
4) Is low in sugars — good.

- Both sandwiches are **low in sugar**, which is **good** because too much sugar is linked to **obesity**.
- Both sandwiches have **medium** levels of **salt** and **total fat**. This is **okay**, but it's not a good idea to eat **a lot** of these products **all of the time** — too much salt is linked to **high blood pressure** and too much fat is linked to **obesity**.
- Sandwich 2 is **less healthy** overall. It's high in **saturated fat**, which can lead to **obesity**, **diabetes** and **heart disease**.

Practice Questions

Q1 What two units do food labels use to show the energy content of the food?
Q2 Suggest why the traffic light system can be more useful than food tables.
Q3 Why could eating foods that are high in salt be bad for you?

Exam Question

Q1 The figure below shows some of the nutritional information taken from the labels of two frozen pizzas:

Pizza A (per pizza)

| Calories 758 | HIGH Fat 40.7 g | HIGH Saturates 21.5 g | LOW Sugar 5 g | HIGH Salt 3.5 g |

Pizza B (per pizza)

| Calories 967 | HIGH Fat 43.5 g | HIGH Saturates 22.5 g | MEDIUM Sugar 7.2 g | HIGH Salt 5 g |

a) Compare the nutritional value of the two pizzas. [6 marks]

b) Suggest one medical condition that could be caused by eating too much of these products. [1 mark]

c) Give two other pieces of information that would be useful in assessing the nutritional value of the pizzas. [2 marks]

The red light district — now in a supermarket near you...

Don't be too scared by all the red circles — it's fine to eat unhealthy food from time to time. Some of this stuff may seem quite obvious — for some foods it's easy to tell whether it's high in fat or sugar without a label. But, sometimes foods may seem healthy but there's hidden fat, sugar and salt — this can be a problem with processed foods. Keep your eyes peeled.

Composition of Food

When you sit down to eat your lunch you're basically munching on bits of other organisms. The molecules they're made of become a part of you. So you really are what you eat... that must make me a ham sandwich and crisps.

Most **Food** we Eat is **From Other Living Organisms**

Most of the **food** we eat is made from **parts of other organisms**, e.g. my nice steak was once part of a cow. These organisms are made from the same types of **biological molecules** as humans are — **fats**, **proteins** and **carbohydrates**.

Miguel never listened to his mum when she told him not to play with his food.

Most **Fats** are Made from **Glycerol** and **Three Fatty Acids**

Most fats are composed of **one** molecule of **glycerol** with **three fatty acid molecules** attached to it. These fats are called **triglycerides**.

Fats are a subgroup of lipids. Other lipids include phospholipids and cholesterol, both found in cell membranes (see p. 22).

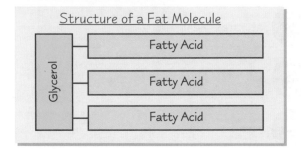

Structure of a Fat Molecule

Glycerol	Fatty Acid
	Fatty Acid
	Fatty Acid

Proteins and Some **Carbohydrates** are **Polymers**

Polymers are made by **joining** together lots of **smaller molecules** called **monomers**.
This table shows the types of monomers that make up the carbohydrates and proteins in our body.

MONOMERS	POLYMER
monosaccharides	carbohydrate (polysaccharide)
amino acids	protein

*When we **digest** our food the reverse happens and the **polymers** are **broken down** into monomers (see p. 12).*

Polymers Are Formed in **Condensation Reactions**

In a **condensation** reaction a **bond** forms between **two monomers** and a molecule of **water** is **released**.

This is an example of a condensation reaction between **two monosaccharides**. The reaction is very similar for **other monomers** — a water molecule is released as a bond forms between them.

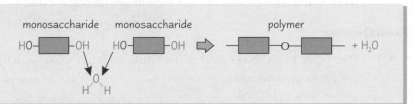

Monosaccharides Form **Disaccharides** and **Polysaccharides**

1) **Single sugar** molecules (e.g. glucose, fructose) are called **monosaccharides**.

2) When **two** monosaccharides join together a **disaccharide** is formed.

3) When **more than two** monosaccharides join together a **polysaccharide** is formed.

4) You need to know the names of some of the molecules formed when glucose molecules link together.

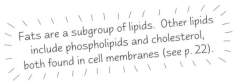

1) **Maltose** — a **disaccharide** made from two glucose molecules.

2) **Starch**
3) **Glycogen** } polysaccharides made from many glucose molecules.
4) **Cellulose**

Composition of Food

Proteins are Made from Long Chains of Amino Acids

1) The **monomers** of proteins are **amino acids**.
2) A **dipeptide** is formed when **two** amino acids join together.
3) A **polypeptide** is formed when **more than two** amino acids join together.
4) **Proteins** are made up of **one or more polypeptides**.

Proteins have a Primary, Secondary and Tertiary Structure

Proteins are **big**, **complicated** molecules. They're easier to explain if you describe their structure in three 'levels'. These levels are called the protein's **primary**, **secondary** and **tertiary** structures.

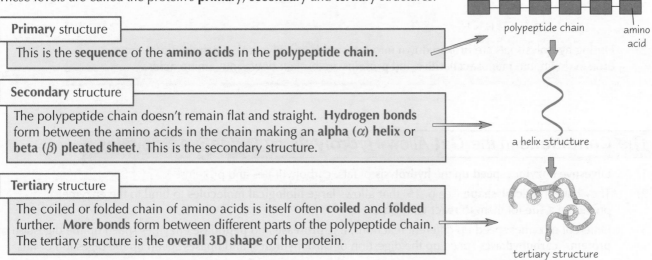

Primary structure

This is the **sequence** of the **amino acids** in the **polypeptide chain**.

polypeptide chain   amino acid

Secondary structure

The polypeptide chain doesn't remain flat and straight. **Hydrogen bonds** form between the amino acids in the chain making an **alpha (α) helix** or **beta (β) pleated sheet**. This is the secondary structure.

a helix structure

Tertiary structure

The coiled or folded chain of amino acids is itself often **coiled** and **folded** further. **More bonds** form between different parts of the polypeptide chain. The tertiary structure is the **overall 3D shape** of the protein.

tertiary structure

The Tertiary Structure is Held Together by Different Types of Bonds

There are **three** types of bonds that hold the tertiary structure together:

1) **Hydrogen bond**
2) **Ionic bond**
3) **Disulfide bridge** (a bond between two sulfur atoms)

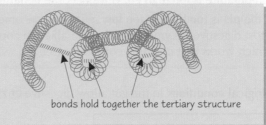

bonds hold together the tertiary structure

Practice Questions

Q1 Name the monomers that make up: i) carbohydrates and ii) proteins.
Q2 Name three polysaccharides of glucose.
Q3 What type of reaction joins together two carbohydrate monomers?

Exam Question

Q1 Describe the structure of a protein, explaining the terms primary, secondary and tertiary structure. Include details of the bonds present in the tertiary structure. [10 marks]

Strong H bonds — hope you're forming many with this revision guide...

The different levels of a protein structure can be hard to imagine. I usually think of a slinky — the wire is the primary structure, it coils up to form the secondary structure and if you coil the slinky round your arm that's the tertiary structure. Oh, I need to get out more. I do wish I had more friends and not just this stupid slinky for company. Slinky, slinky, slinky.

Digestion of Food and Chromatography

So you know what a balanced diet is, what happens if you don't eat a balanced diet and how to spot healthy food from a mile off. Now it's time to take a look at what happens to food when you eat it.

Food is **Broken Down** into **Smaller Molecules** during **Digestion**

1) The **large biological molecules** (e.g. polymers) in food are **insoluble**.

2) During digestion they're **broken down** into **smaller molecules** (e.g. monomers), which are **soluble** and are **easily absorbed** from the gut into the blood, to be **used** by the body.

3) This is done by **hydrolysis reactions**, which **break** bonds by **adding water**.

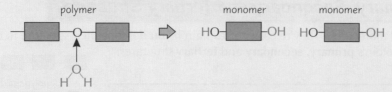

During hydrolysis fats are broken down into **fatty acids** and **glycerol**. **Carbohydrates** are broken down into **monosaccharides** and **proteins** are broken down into **amino acids**.

The **Conditions** in the **Gut** Allow **Hydrolysis** by **Digestive Enzymes**

1) Digestive enzymes **speed up** the **hydrolysis** of fats, carbohydrates and proteins.

2) They have a **specific shape** (see p. 15) that allows **large biological molecules** to **bind** to the enzyme, providing a **site** for them to **react** with **water**.

3) Different enzymes speed up different reactions, e.g. **protease** and **peptidase** enzymes speed up the digestion of **proteins**, **carbohydrases** speed up the digestion of **carbohydrates**, and **lipases** speed up the digestion of **fats**.

> Enzymes (see p. 16 for more) **work best** at the **right temperature** and **pH**:
>
> 1) If the **temperature** is **too low** there won't be enough energy for reactions to occur. If the temperature is **too high** enzymes become **denatured** (lose their shape) and stop working properly.
>
> 2) If the **pH** is **too high** or **too low**, enzymes become **denatured** and stop working properly. Most digestive enzymes work best in **alkaline** conditions (pH > 7). One exception is **pepsin**, which works best in **acidic** conditions (see below).

The **physiological conditions** in the gut allow digestive enzymes to work effectively.

Sometimes the digestive system is referred to as the gut.

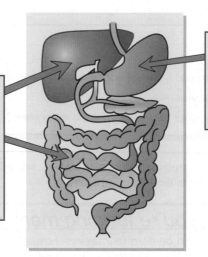

1) **Body temperature** is **37 °C** — this is warm enough for digestive enzymes to work quickly.

3) The **liver** produces **bile**, which neutralises stomach acid. This creates **alkaline** conditions in the small intestine needed for other digestive enzymes, e.g. carbohydrases and lipases, to work.

2) The **stomach** produces **hydrochloric acid**, which creates the acidic conditions needed for the enzyme **pepsin** to work.

Digestion of Food and Chromatography

Chromatography Separates Out Components in a Mixture

If you have a **mixture** of biological molecules in a sample that you want to test, you can often **separate** and **purify** them using **chromatography**. For example, you may want to find out about the different molecules present in a particular food colouring. Here's how you do it:

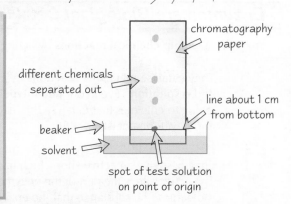

Scientists can use chromatography to separate and identify proteins in a cell sample.

1) Draw a **pencil line** across a strip of **chromatography paper**, about 1 cm from the bottom — this is the baseline.

2) Put a spot of the **test solution** onto a point along the baseline — this is the **point of origin**.

3) Put the chromatography paper into a beaker with some **solvent** (e.g. water, ethanol), making sure the baseline stays **above the solvent**.

4) As the solvent spreads up the paper, the different chemicals in the test solution move with it, but at **different rates** (due to different solubilities), so they separate out.

chromatography paper

different chemicals separated out

line about 1 cm from bottom

beaker

solvent

spot of test solution on point of origin

Components in a Mixture Can be Identified Using R_f Values

1) You can identify what the separated molecules are using their **R_f values**.

2) Each different type of molecule has a different R_f value.

R_f values are always less than 1 and they're specific to the particular solvent used.

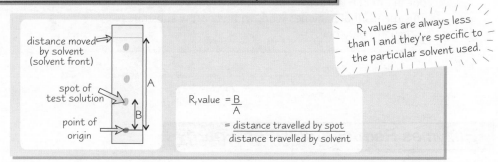

distance moved by solvent (solvent front)

spot of test solution

A

point of origin

B

$$R_f \text{ value} = \frac{B}{A}$$

$$= \frac{\text{distance travelled by spot}}{\text{distance travelled by solvent}}$$

Practice Questions

Q1 What is a hydrolysis reaction?

Q2 What are the conditions in the gut that enable most digestive enzymes to work?

Q3 How is the R_f value of a chemical calculated?

Exam Question

Q1 The table below shows properties of some of the digestive enzymes produced by the body:

Enzyme	Hydrolyses	Products of hydrolysis	Conditions required	Location of reaction
pepsin	protein		acidic	
lipase	fat			small intestine
carbohydrase	carbohydrate	monosaccharides		

a) Complete the table. [6 marks]

b) Explain how the stomach and the liver affect the pH of the digestive system. [2 marks]

c) Explain what happens during hydrolysis and why it is important during digestion. [3 marks]

Chocolate biccies speed up the rate of revision...

All this stuff might seem quite boring but enzymes are useful little things. They're used to make beer, bread, biological detergents, cheeses, paper and even fruit juices... and if that wasn't enough they also help you digest all that food you eat. Luckily for you Section 2 is all about enzymes — now the fun can really begin...

Action of Enzymes

Enzymes are dead important — they crop up loads in biology. You may remember them from the last section, and they'll probably make another couple of appearances before the end of this book. This entire section's dedicated to enzymes — how they work, how we make them work for us, and what happens when they go wrong. So, fasten your seatbelts and tie your shoelaces — this promises to be a roller coaster ride of fast, specific, catalytic fun.

Enzymes are Biological Catalysts

Enzymes **speed up chemical reactions** by acting as **biological catalysts**.

1) They catalyse **metabolic reactions** in your body, e.g. **digestion** and **respiration**. Even your **phenotype** (physical appearance) is due to enzymes that catalyse the reactions that cause growth and development (see p. 48).

2) Enzymes are **proteins**.

3) Enzymes have an **active site**, which has a **specific shape**. The active site is the part of the enzyme where the **substrate** molecules (the substance that the enzyme interacts with) **bind to**.

4) For the enzyme to work, the substrate has to **fit into** the **active site** (its shape has to be **complementary**). If the substrate shape doesn't match the active site, the reaction won't be catalysed. This means that enzymes work with very few substrates — usually only one.

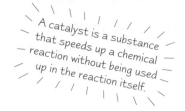
A catalyst is a substance that speeds up a chemical reaction without being used up in the reaction itself.

Dave knew Sara was a lovely girl, but just couldn't get past the shape incompatibility thing.

Enzymes Reduce Activation Energy

In a chemical reaction, a certain amount of energy needs to be supplied to the reactants before the reaction will start. This is called the **activation energy** — it's often provided as **heat**.

Enzymes **reduce** the amount of activation energy needed, often making reactions happen at a **lower temperature** than without an enzyme. This **speeds** up the **rate of reaction**.

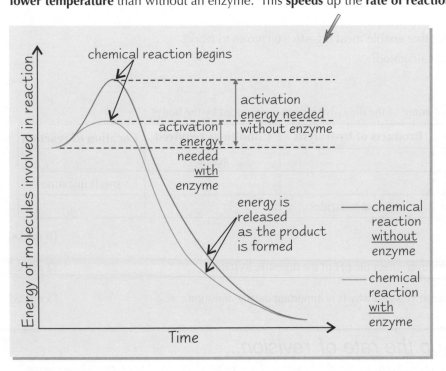

When a substance binds to an enzyme's active site, an **enzyme-substrate complex** is formed. It's the formation of the enzyme-substrate complex that **lowers** the **activation energy**. Here are two reasons why:

1) If two substrate molecules need to be **joined**, attaching to the enzyme holds them **close together**, **reducing** any **repulsion** between the molecules so they can bond more easily.

2) If the enzyme is catalysing a **breakdown reaction**, fitting into the active site puts a **strain** on bonds in the substrate. This strain means the substrate molecule **breaks up** more easily.

Action of Enzymes

The 'Lock and Key' Model is a Good Start...

Enzymes are a bit picky — they only work with substrates that fit their active site.
Early scientists studying the action of enzymes came up with the 'lock and key' model.
This is where the **substrate fits** into the **enzyme** in the same way that a **key fits** into a **lock**.

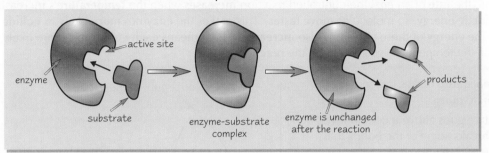

The 'Luminous Tights' model
was popular in the 1980s
but has since been found to
be grossly inappropriate.

Scientists soon realised that the lock and key model didn't give the full story. The enzyme and substrate
do have to fit together in the first place, but new evidence showed that the **enzyme-substrate complex
changed shape** slightly to complete the fit. This **locks** the substrate even more tightly to the enzyme.
Scientists modified the old lock and key model and came up with the **'induced fit'** model.

*...but the 'Induced Fit' Model is a **Better Theory***

The **'induced fit'** model helps to explain why enzymes are so **specific** and only bond to one particular substrate.
The substrate doesn't only have to be the right shape to fit the active site, it has to make the active site **change shape**
in the right way as well. This is a prime example of how a widely accepted theory can **change** when **new evidence**
comes along. The 'induced fit' model is still widely accepted — for now, anyway.

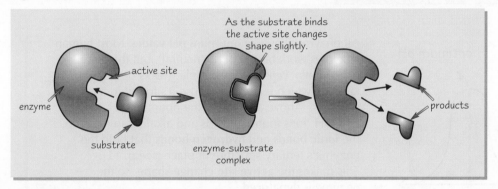

Practice Questions

Q1   What is an enzyme?

Q2   What is the name given to the amount of energy needed to start a reaction?

Q3   What is an enzyme-substrate complex?

Q4   Explain why enzymes are specific.

Exam Question

Q1   Describe the 'lock and key' model of enzyme action and explain how the 'induced fit' model is different.   [7 marks]

Porridge and two slices of toast — that's my activation energy...

*OK, nothing too tricky here. Enzymes are proteins that catalyse metabolic reactions. Every enzyme has a specific active
site shape, so it only works with substrates that fit the shape. Everyone used to think that the lock and key model
explained everything but, like most things, it's been replaced with a newer and more spangly model — induced fit.*

Enzyme Activity and Digestive Enzymes

Now you know what enzymes are and how they work, it's time to take a look at what makes them tick. Humans need things like money, caffeine and the newest mobile phone but enzymes are quite content with the right temperature and pH.

Temperature *has a* Big Influence *on Enzyme Activity*

Like any chemical reaction, the **rate** of an enzyme-controlled reaction **increases** when the **temperature's increased**. More heat means **more kinetic energy**, so molecules **move faster**. This makes the enzymes **more likely** to **collide** with the substrate molecules. The **energy** of these collisions also **increases**, which means each collision is more likely to **result** in a **reaction**. But, if the temperature gets too high, the **reaction stops**.

1) The rise in temperature makes the enzyme's molecules **vibrate more**.

2) If the temperature goes above a certain level, this vibration **breaks** some of the **bonds** that hold the enzyme in shape.

3) The **active site changes shape** and the enzyme and substrate **no longer fit together**.

4) At this point, the enzyme is **denatured** — it no longer functions as a catalyst.

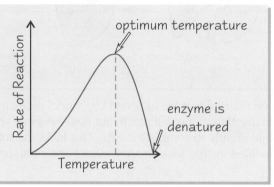

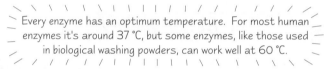

Every enzyme has an optimum temperature. For most human enzymes it's around 37 °C, but some enzymes, like those used in biological washing powders, can work well at 60 °C.

pH *Also Affects Enzyme Activity*

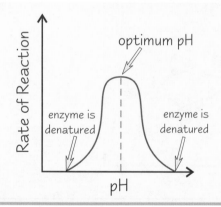

All enzymes have an **optimum pH value**. Most human enzymes work best at pH 7 (neutral), but there are exceptions. **Pepsin**, for example, works best at pH 2 (acidic), which is useful because it's found in the stomach. Above and below the optimum pH, the H^+ and OH^- ions found in acids and alkalis can mess up the **ionic bonds** and **hydrogen bonds** that hold the enzyme's tertiary structure in place (see p. 11). This makes the **active site change shape**, so the enzyme is **denatured**.

Substrate Concentration *Affects the Rate of Reaction* Up to a Point

The **higher** the substrate concentration, the **faster** the reaction — more substrate molecules means a **collision** between substrate and enzyme is **more likely** and so more active sites will be used. This is only true up until a **'saturation' point** though. After that, there are so many substrate molecules that the enzymes have about as much as they can cope with (all the **active sites are full**), and adding more **makes no difference**.

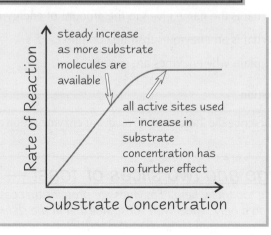

Enzyme Activity and Digestive Enzymes

Enzymes are Important in Digestion

Many **digestive enzymes** are produced by our bodies (see p. 12). Each one is **specific** to a certain reaction — the shape of the enzyme only allows one type of molecule to attach to it. So, if your body doesn't produce an enzyme to digest a particular substance, you **won't be able** to **digest** that substance. Take a look at the following example.

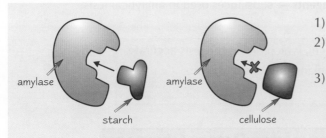

1) **Starch** and **cellulose** are different types of carbohydrate.

2) Our bodies produce the enzyme **amylase**, which speeds up the digestion of **starch** into simple sugars.

3) Because **cellulose doesn't fit** into the active site of amylase, and because we don't produce any enzymes that cellulose will fit into, we're **unable** to digest it.

In the exam you could be asked **why** our bodies can't digest certain chemicals. Whatever the chemical is, the answer will always be the **same** — we can't digest something if we **don't produce** an enzyme with an active site the right shape to fit the chemical. Simple as that.

Lactose Intolerance is Caused by the Lack of an Enzyme

1) **Lactose** is a **sugar** found in milk.

2) It's digested by an **enzyme** called **lactase**, found in the intestines.

3) If you **don't** have enough of the enzyme lactase, you won't be able to break down the lactose in milk properly — a condition called **lactose intolerance**.

4) Undigested lactose is fermented by bacteria and can cause a whole host of **intestinal complaints** such as **stomach cramps**, excessive **flatulence** (wind) and **diarrhoea**.

5) Milk can be artificially treated with purified lactase to make it suitable for lactose-intolerant people.

6) It's fairly uncommon to be lactose tolerant though — around 15% of Northern Europeans, 50% of Mediterraneans, 95% of Asians and 90% of people of African descent are lactose intolerant.

Practice Questions

Q1 What does it mean if an enzyme is denatured?

Q2 Explain why increasing the concentration of a substrate doesn't always increase the rate of reaction.

Q3 Explain why our bodies can digest starch but not cellulose.

Q4 What happens if our bodies don't produce enough of the enzyme lactase?

Exam Questions

Q1 When doing an experiment with enzymes, explain why it is necessary to control the temperature and pH of the solutions involved. [8 marks]

Q2 'Sug-stitute' is an artificial sweetener. It's used in food and drink as a low-calorie alternative to sugar. The sweetener contains a chemical that is not digested by our bodies. Suggest why the chemical cannot be digested. [2 marks]

People without toes make me windy — I've got lack-toes intolerance...

It's not easy being an enzyme. They're just trying to get on with their jobs, but the whole world seems to be against them sometimes. High temperature, wrong pH — they're all out to get them. And if those poor enzymes didn't exist we couldn't survive. Sad though it is, make sure you know every word. Learn how different factors affect enzyme activity, and be able to describe why we can't digest cellulose. (Or any other substance, because the answer will be the same...)

Enzymes in Medicine

Not satisfied with a life in the intestines, some enzymes aim for the top and a career in medicine — kind of. The special properties of enzymes mean they can be used in diagnosing and treating diseases. But sometimes enzymes can have an adverse effect on the body — causing more harm than good. Ooh, this section has more twists than some trashy novel.

Enzymes can be used to Detect Specific Chemicals

Enzymes' properties mean they can be used as **analytical reagents** — substances used in analytical tests.
Enzymes are useful because:

1) They're **specific** (they only bind to one test substance), which makes the tests **accurate**.
2) They react with **low concentrations** of substrate, making the tests **sensitive**.
3) They **work quickly**.

Glucose Oxidase and Peroxidase can be used to Detect Glucose

It's possible to diagnose **diabetes** (see p. 6) by testing a person's urine for **glucose**. Normally, the urine **doesn't** contain any glucose. Testing for glucose involves dipping a special strip in urine. The strip has a coloured square at one end that's impregnated with two enzymes, **glucose oxidase** and **peroxidase**, and a **pink dye**.

1) Glucose oxidase is an enzyme that catalyses the reaction between glucose, oxygen and water.

glucose + oxygen + water → gluconic acid + hydrogen peroxide

If glucose is present in the urine, hydrogen peroxide is produced.

2) Hydrogen peroxide reacts with the pink dye, causing a **colour change** (to blue). The reaction between the pink dye and hydrogen peroxide is catalysed by the enzyme peroxidase.

hydrogen peroxide + pink dye → blue dye + water

So, if the strip **turns blue** when it's dipped into a sample of urine, **glucose is present**. If it stays pink then glucose isn't present.

Lung Disease can be Caused by Enzymes

1) **Emphysema** is a lung disease caused by **damage** to a protein called **elastin**.
2) Elastin is present in **alveoli** in the lungs (see page 20). It's **elastic**, which allows the alveoli to return to their **normal shape** after inhaling and exhaling air.
3) Without elastin alveoli **collapse**, resulting in difficulty breathing and hyperventilation (quick, shallow breaths).
4) It's often caused by **smoking**, but can also be caused by a **hereditary disorder** where you have a **deficiency** in a protein called **alpha-1-antitrypsin**.

- **Alpha-1-antitrypsin** is produced in the liver and circulates in the bloodstream.
- One of its jobs is to **inhibit** the action of the **enzyme elastase**.
- Elastase **breaks down elastin**. It has the potential to damage the elastin in **healthy lung tissue** but, when it's inhibited by alpha-1-antitrypsin, it only breaks down **old** or **damaged tissue**.

5) So, if you **don't have enough alpha-1-antitrypsin**, elastase **isn't inhibited** and slowly breaks down elastin in the lungs, leading to **emphysema**.
6) Luckily, the deficiency can be treated with **intravenous injections** of alpha-1-antitrypsin.

Enzymes in Medicine

Enzyme Replacement Therapy can be used to Treat Cystic Fibrosis Symptoms

Cystic fibrosis (see page 21) is a hereditary disease caused by a faulty gene. The disease causes **thick mucus** to be produced in the **lungs** and the **digestive system**. Most people with cystic fibrosis have **difficulty digesting** foods because the tube from the pancreas to the small intestines gets **blocked**, so enzymes produced in the pancreas **can't reach** the small intestine.

1) **Pancreatic Enzyme Replacement Therapy (PERT)** can be used to help cystic fibrosis sufferers digest food.
2) Patients are given **artificial enzymes** (including proteases, carbohydrases and lipases) to **replace** the digestive enzymes normally released by the pancreas.
3) The enzymes are administered in capsules and are usually taken before or with a meal.
4) People with cystic fibrosis are then able to **digest** and **absorb** proteins, carbohydrates and fats, and to eat a greater range of foods without experiencing digestive discomfort.

Pancreatitis Affects Enzyme Levels in the Blood and Gut

Pancreatitis is an **inflammation** of the **pancreas**. It can be caused by a number of things — for example by **gallstones** (crystalline deposits in the body) or by **excessive alcohol consumption**.

1) The **digestive enzymes** secreted by the pancreas aren't usually **activated** until they reach the digestive system. If someone is suffering from pancreatitis, the enzymes become active **too early** and begin to digest the pancreas itself.
2) As bits of the pancreas are **killed off** its ability to produce enzymes is affected — this results in changes in the **concentration** and **distribution** of enzymes in the body. It can cause an **increase** in the concentration of digestive enzymes in the **blood**, or a **decrease** in the concentration of these enzymes in the **gut**.
3) This can result in **digestive problems**, **abdominal pain**, **nausea** and **vomiting**.
4) People with pancreatitis usually have to eat a **specially designed diet** and take **pain-relieving drugs**.

Practice Questions

Q1 Give three reasons why enzymes make good analytical reagents.

Q2 Which protein protects lung tissue from the damaging effects of elastase?

Q3 Describe one example of enzyme replacement therapy.

Q4 What is pancreatitis?

Exam Questions

Q1 Testing urine for glucose using reagent strips is a simple, non-invasive method of detecting and monitoring diabetes.

a) Describe the role of glucose oxidase and peroxidase in testing for glucose. [4 marks]

b) Explain why this test will detect glucose, but not other simple sugars. [2 marks]

Q2 Explain how alpha-1-antitrypsin deficiency can lead to emphysema. [3 marks]

Q3 Explain why pancreatitis often results in digestive problems, and suggest one way of treating the disorder. [3 marks]

Being dunked in wee — just what an enzyme always wanted to do...

Pancreatitis is a pretty grim disease, unless you enjoy nausea and vomiting that is. Acute pancreatitis affects around 20 000 people a year in the UK, and that number's on the up. Gallstones are the most common cause of pancreatitis, but binge drinking is doing its bit too. Make sure you know all about pancreatitis, just in case it rears its ugly head in the exam.

Gas Exchange

Cystic fibrosis is a hereditary disease that affects gas exchange in the lungs. So it's probably going to be pretty useful if you know how gas exchange and all that works...

Lungs are Specialised Organs for Ventilation

Humans need to get **oxygen** into the blood and get rid of **carbon dioxide** — this is where **breathing** (or **ventilation** as it's sometimes called) and the **lungs** come in.

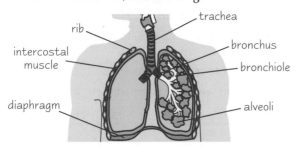

rib
intercostal muscle
diaphragm
trachea
bronchus
bronchiole
alveoli

1) As we breathe in, air enters the **trachea** (windpipe).

2) The trachea splits into two **bronchi** — one **bronchus** leading to each lung.

3) Each bronchus then branches off into smaller tubes called **bronchioles**.

4) The bronchioles end in small 'air sacs' called **alveoli**.

5) The **ribs**, **diaphragm** and **intercostal muscles** all work together to move air in and out.

Gas Exchange Occurs in the Alveoli

Alveoli are microscopic air sacs where **gas exchange** occurs. Each **alveolus** (single air sac) is surrounded by a **single layer of cells** — the **epithelium**. Most vessels and tissues inside our body are lined with an epithelium.

Oxygen (O_2) diffuses **out of** the alveolar space, across the **alveolar epithelium** and the **capillary endothelium** (a type of epithelium that forms the capillary wall), and into the **blood**.

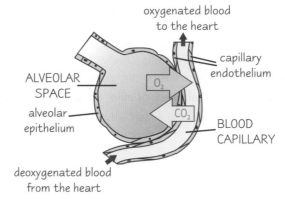

oxygenated blood to the heart
capillary endothelium
ALVEOLAR SPACE
O_2
CO_2
alveolar epithelium
BLOOD CAPILLARY
deoxygenated blood from the heart

Carbon dioxide (CO_2) diffuses **into** the **alveolar space** from the blood and is **breathed out**.

The air space inside the alveolus is called the alveolar space.

Gas Exchange Involves Diffusion

Gases move into and out of the alveoli by **diffusion**.

1) Diffusion is the net movement of particles (molecules or ions) from an area of **higher concentration** to an area of **lower concentration**. This continues until particles are **evenly distributed** throughout the liquid or gas.

2) Diffusion is described as a **passive process** — **no energy** is needed for it to happen.

3) The rate of diffusion is affected by **surface area**, the **length of the diffusion pathway** (distance) and the **concentration gradient**.

Lungs Are Efficient Gas Exchange Organs

Gas exchange in the lungs is **efficient** because there is:

1) A **large surface area** — the **huge number** of alveoli means there's a large surface area for gas exchange.

2) A **short diffusion pathway** — alveoli have a **thin epithelium**, and capillaries have a **thin endothelium**.

3) A **large concentration gradient** — there's a steep concentration gradient of respiratory gases between the **alveoli** and the **blood capillaries**.

Lucy hoped no one else would notice her sister's gas exchange...

Gas Exchange

The **Concentration Gradient** is **Maintained** by **Ventilation**

After passing oxygen on to the body's cells, **deoxygenated blood** returns to the **lungs** to pick up **more oxygen**.

1) There's a **higher** concentration of O_2 in the **alveolar spaces** than in the blood capillaries. The large concentration gradient causes **oxygen** to diffuse into the **blood**.

2) There's a **lower** concentration of CO_2 in the **alveolar spaces** than in the blood capillaries. CO_2 **diffuses** down the concentration gradient and **into the lungs**.

3) **Ventilation** brings O_2 into the lungs and takes CO_2 out, maintaining the **concentration gradient** of the gases.

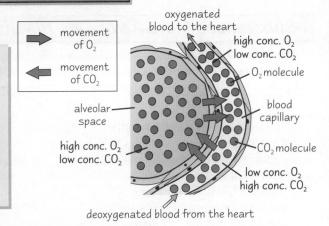

movement of O_2

movement of CO_2

oxygenated blood to the heart

high conc. O_2 low conc. CO_2

O_2 molecule

alveolar space

blood capillary

high conc. O_2 low conc. CO_2

CO_2 molecule

low conc. O_2 high conc. CO_2

deoxygenated blood from the heart

Gas Exchange is **Impaired** in People with **Cystic Fibrosis**

Everyone has **mucus** in their lungs — it helps to **prevent infection** (see below). People with cystic fibrosis (**CF**) have especially **thick** mucus, which impairs gas exchange.

The epithelium lining our **upper respiratory tract** (trachea, bronchi and bronchioles) contains two special types of cells — **goblet cells** and **ciliated cells**.

Goblet cells also line our gut and release mucus to lubricate it.

1) Goblet cells **secrete mucus** onto the surface of the epithelium. Mucus is made up of **glycoproteins** (proteins with carbohydrate molecules attached to them). Its job is to **trap particles** present in **inhaled air**, preventing them from entering the **smaller bronchioles** and **alveoli**, where they could cause an **infection**.

2) **Ciliated cells** are epithelial cells with **hair-like structures** (called **cilia**) on their surface. The cilia **beat** (move backwards and forwards) to waft the mucus up, **away** from the **lungs** and **towards** the **throat**. Here, the mucus may be **coughed up** and **spat out**, or **swallowed** and **digested** in the stomach.

In people suffering from CF their mucus is **thick** and **sticky**. **Cilia** can't waft it upwards, so the mucus **builds up** in their airways. This **reduces the efficiency of gas exchange** in two ways:

1) The **volume** of air able to get in and out of the lungs is much **lower** because the passages are narrower, so the **concentration gradient** is **decreased**.

2) A 'mucus plug' may form. This is where mucus completely **blocks** an airway. It prevents air from **reaching** a whole section of **alveoli** and **decreases** the **concentration gradient** across them.

Practice Questions

Q1 Give two factors that affect the rate of diffusion.

Q2 How is the concentration gradient of O_2 and CO_2 maintained in the alveoli?

Q3 What is the role of mucus in our lungs?

Exam Questions

Q1 Explain why the lungs are efficient gas exchange organs. [6 marks]

Q2 Explain how the efficiency of gas exchange is reduced in someone suffering from cystic fibrosis. [4 marks]

A large concentration gradient — is what's needed to absorb this page...

OK, take a deep breath in... and out. Then consider what would happen if air didn't keep entering your lungs by ventilation — the concentration gradient wouldn't be high enough for much oxygen to diffuse into the blood. So, to cut a long story short, you'd be in a bit of a pickle. Good job we don't have to remember to breathe...

Mucus Production

We've all got mucus in our lungs, but it's too thick in people with CF, which causes problems. So now I bet you're thinking — what causes mucus to be thin and runny, or thick and sticky? Oh, you weren't thinking that... oh well...

Substances Move Across the Plasma Membranes of Cells

Mucus contains water and solutes (ions or molecules). The water and solutes enter the mucus via the **plasma membranes** of surrounding cells. All the body's cells are surrounded by plasma membranes. They're composed of **lipids** (mainly phospholipids), **proteins** and **carbohydrates** (which are usually attached to proteins or lipids).

The **fluid mosaic model** describes the arrangement of molecules in the membrane. **Phospholipid molecules** form a continuous, double layer (**called a bilayer**). This layer is 'fluid' because the phospholipids are constantly moving. **Protein molecules** are scattered through the layer, like tiles in a **mosaic**.

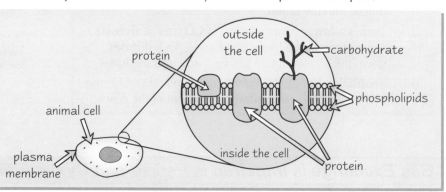

One of the functions of cell membranes is to control **which substances enter and leave** a cell. Substances can pass across the plasma membrane either by **diffusion** (see p. 20), **osmosis** or **active transport**. Plasma membranes are **partially permeable** — they let some molecules through but not others.

Water Molecules Cross Plasma Membranes by Osmosis

Like diffusion, osmosis is **passive** — it **doesn't** require any **energy**. Here's how it works:

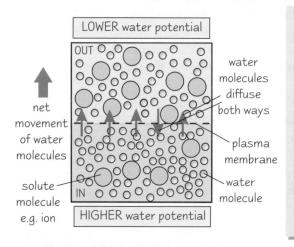

1) Osmosis is the **diffusion** of **water molecules** across a **partially permeable membrane**, from an area of **higher water potential** (i.e. higher concentration of water molecules) to an area of **lower water potential** (i.e. lower concentration of water molecules).

2) **Water potential** is the potential (likelihood) of water molecules to diffuse out of or into a solution.

3) Water molecules are small and can diffuse easily through the **plasma membrane**, but large solute molecules can't.

4) Water molecules will diffuse **both ways** through the membrane, but the **net movement** will be to the side with the **lower water potential** (lower concentration of water molecules).

Some Substances Cross Plasma Membranes by Active Transport

Active transport uses **energy** to move **molecules** and **ions** across plasma membranes, **against a concentration gradient**. This process usually involves membrane proteins, called **carrier proteins**. Carrier proteins transport solutes across the membrane by undergoing a **change in shape**. Here's one in action:

1) A **solute**, e.g. calcium, **attaches** to a specific **carrier protein** in the plasma membrane of a cell.

2) The carrier protein **changes shape** (its tertiary structure — see p. 11 — is altered).

3) This moves the calcium ion **across** the membrane, **releasing it** on the other side.

4) **Energy**, from ATP (adenosine triphosphate — a common source of energy used in the cell), is used to move the solute against its concentration gradient.

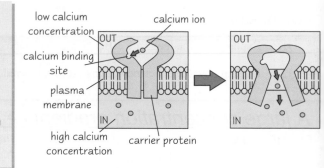

Mucus Production

CF Sufferers Have a Defective CFTR Membrane Protein

The **goblet cells** that line our **lungs** also line our **gut**. These goblet cells contain the **CFTR** (Cystic Fibrosis Transmembrane Conductance Regulator) **protein**. This protein is involved in **making mucus**. CF sufferers have a **mutation** in the **gene** coding for the CFTR protein. This results in a **defective CFTR protein** and **thick, sticky** mucus.

The **CFTR protein** is a **plasma membrane protein**. The function of this protein is to **pump chloride ions out** of the cell, by **active transport**, into the mucus. As the number of chloride ions in the mucus **increases**, the concentration of water molecules in the mucus **decreases** — the mucus now has a **lower water potential** than the cell. This causes **water to move out of the cell** and **into the mucus**, by osmosis, making the mucus **more fluid**.

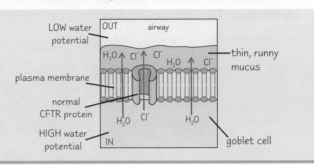

In people with CF, the **defective form** of the CFTR protein has an **altered tertiary structure** — it **can't** transport chloride ions out of the cell. Chloride ions are **trapped** inside the cell, lowering the water potential inside the cell. The cell now has a **lower water potential** than the mucus, so **water is retained** instead of moving out by osmosis. This causes the mucus to become **dehydrated** and **sticky**, making it difficult for the cilia to move it upwards — the mucus **accumulates** and **thickens**.

People suffering from CF have a persistent cough, as the lungs try to remove the heavy mucus. Sufferers may have daily physiotherapy to help loosen the thick, sticky mucus, so it can be removed from the lungs.

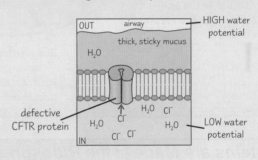

People With CF Are More Prone to Lung Infections

1) We **breathe in bacteria** all the time. They don't usually cause much harm because they get **stuck** in the **mucus** in our airways, which is coughed up or swallowed (the bacteria are **killed** by the **stomach acid**).

2) People with CF can't get rid of the thick mucus. **Trapped bacteria** have time to **multiply** in the **warm, moist** and **nutrient-rich** mucus. **Large numbers** of bacteria can cause serious **infections**, like pneumonia.

3) It's also difficult for **immune system cells** (see p. 32) to penetrate the thick mucus and kill the bacteria.

4) When the immune system does start to fight an infection in the lungs, it can cause **inflammation**. This narrows the airways and makes it even more difficult for people with CF to **breathe**.

Practice Questions

Q1   What is osmosis?

Q2   What is the function of the CFTR protein?

Exam Questions

Q1   Explain how a defective CFTR protein results in thick, sticky mucus.   [8 marks]

Q2   Explain why a person with cystic fibrosis is more prone to lung infections.   [4 marks]

Fluid Mosaic Model — think I saw one being sold at a craft fair...

You need to learn everything on the page... phlegm and all. Don't forget that ions and molecules lower water potential (the concentration of water molecules), and that water molecules tend to move to an area of lower water potential. If you get a bit confused about water potential try replacing the word 'potential' with 'concentration' and it'll become clearer.

Mucus Production

The CFTR protein and glycoproteins (see page 21) are both needed to produce mucus.
So, here's how our bodies make them...

Many Organelles Are Involved in Making Proteins like CFTR

An **organelle** is a **structure** found inside a **cell**. Each organelle has a **specific function** and most are surrounded by **membranes**. Here's some info about the ones needed to make proteins:

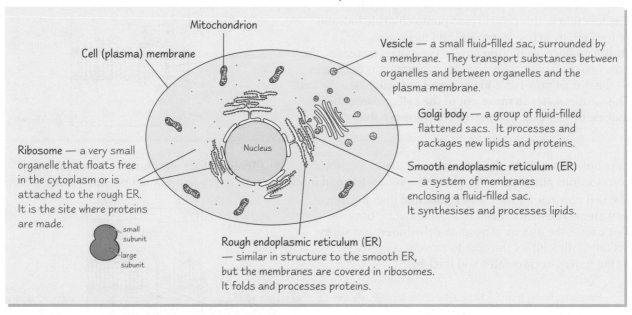

Cell (plasma) membrane

Mitochondrion

Nucleus

Vesicle — a small fluid-filled sac, surrounded by a membrane. They transport substances between organelles and between organelles and the plasma membrane.

Golgi body — a group of fluid-filled flattened sacs. It processes and packages new lipids and proteins.

Smooth endoplasmic reticulum (ER) — a system of membranes enclosing a fluid-filled sac. It synthesises and processes lipids.

Ribosome — a very small organelle that floats free in the cytoplasm or is attached to the rough ER. It is the site where proteins are made.

small subunit

large subunit

Rough endoplasmic reticulum (ER) — similar in structure to the smooth ER, but the membranes are covered in ribosomes. It folds and processes proteins.

Proteins are Made at the Ribosomes

1) Proteins are **made** at the **ribosomes** in the cytoplasm and at the ribosomes on the rough ER. The **CFTR protein** and **glycoproteins** found in **mucus** are made by ribosomes on the rough ER.

2) First they're **folded** and **processed** (e.g. sugar chains are added) in the **rough ER**.

3) Then the proteins are **transported** from the ER to the **Golgi body** in **vesicles**.

4) At the Golgi body, the proteins may undergo **further processing** (e.g. sugar chains are trimmed or more are added).

5) The proteins enter more **vesicles** to be transported around the cell.

   • The glycoproteins found in mucus move to the cell surface and are **secreted**.

   • The CFTR proteins are **inserted** into the **plasma membrane**.

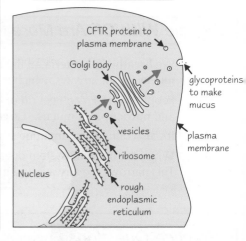

Protein Production in a Cell

CFTR protein to plasma membrane

Golgi body

glycoproteins to make mucus

vesicles

plasma membrane

ribosome

Nucleus

rough endoplasmic reticulum

Protein Production Needs ATP Produced by Mitochondria

Making proteins requires **energy**, usually supplied by **adenosine triphosphate** (ATP). Many other cellular processes require **ATP**, including **active transport** (e.g. of chloride ions by the **CFTR protein**).
ATP is produced in organelles called **mitochondria**, which is where **respiration** takes place.
Cells that need a lot of energy contain a large number of mitochondria.

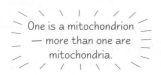

One is a mitochondrion — more than one are mitochondria.

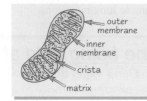

outer membrane

inner membrane

crista

matrix

Mitochondria are usually oval in shape. They have a **double membrane** — the inner one is folded to form structures called **cristae**. Inside is the **matrix**, which contains enzymes involved in respiration.

Mucus Production

CF Sufferers Have Thick, Sticky Mucus in Their Gut

As well as breathing problems, CF sufferers also have difficulty **digesting food**.
This is because of the **thick**, **sticky mucus** they produce.

We All Have Mucus in Our Gut

Goblet cells, like the ones in our airways, can also be found in our digestive system — around the pancreas and duodenum. The **mucus** produced by goblet cells in our gut (see p. 21) helps to **protect** the gut wall from being broken down by our digestive enzymes. It also **lubricates** the gut wall, helping food to slide along easily.

Thick Mucus Blocks Digestive Enzymes

The pancreas releases **digestive enzymes** into the **small intestine**. In people with CF, these enzymes can't get through the thick, sticky mucus that blocks the **duct** leading to the **small intestine**. This means **food isn't broken down** properly. **Nutrients** can't be absorbed and **vitamins** and **minerals** remain **trapped** in undigested food.

Food absorption is also decreased because **mucus** blocks the release of substances from **glands** in the **duodenum**. These substances **neutralise stomach acid** — if they aren't present the **lining** of the duodenum may be **damaged** by the acid.

People with CF may show symptoms like **weight loss** and **nutritional deficiencies** because they aren't getting the nutrients they need. They may also pass grey, smelly **faeces** due to the undigested **fats** that remain in their bowels. CF sufferers are also at greater risk of **diabetes** because trapped enzymes may start to **digest** the pancreas, reducing its ability to release **insulin**.

CF Sufferers Take Enzyme Capsules to Help them Digest Food

CF patients are often given **enzyme capsules**. These capsules are taken with each meal and contain **pancreatic enzymes** needed for digestion.

- **lipase** — to help digest fats
- **protease** — to help digest proteins
- **amylase** — to help digest starch

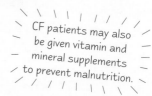
CF patients may also be given vitamin and mineral supplements to prevent malnutrition.

Practice Questions

Q1 Which organelle transports substances between organelles and the plasma membrane?
Q2 What is the function of mitochondria?
Q3 Why is mucus needed in the gut?
Q4 Name three enzymes present in enzyme capsules taken by CF sufferers.

Exam Questions

Q1 Describe the role of the different organelles involved in the production of the CFTR protein. [6 marks]

Q2 Explain why a person with cystic fibrosis may have:

a) a nutritional deficiency. [2 marks]

b) a damaged pancreas. [2 marks]

Revisionase — take one capsule before you read this page...

Organelles are surrounded by a membrane, but they're not cells — just parts of a cell. Don't get confused if they give you a weirdy close-up diagram in the exam. Make sure you learn how they're involved in making CFTR and mucus glycoproteins. I never realised quite how complicated making phlegm was... I've got a whole new appreciation now.

Bacteria

Disease can be caused by microorganisms (e.g. bacteria and viruses). Some bacteria and all viruses are pathogens (organisms that cause disease). They use us for their growth and reproduction, which is a bit gross if you think about it...

Bacteria are Prokaryotes

There are **two** types of cell — **prokaryotic** and **eukaryotic**.

1)   Eukaryotic cells are **complex** and include all **animal** and **plant cells**.

2)   Prokaryotic cells are **smaller** and **simpler**.

3)   Bacteria are single **prokaryotic cells**, so they're called **prokaryotes**.

See p. 24 for more on organelles.

You need to know the **structure** of a prokaryotic cell and what all the different organelles inside are for.

The **flagellum** (plural **flagella**) is a long, hair-like structure that rotates to make the bacterium **move**. But, **not all** bacteria have one.

Ribosomes are the site of **protein synthesis**. In prokaryotic cells, they're free in the cytoplasm.

The **cell (plasma) membrane** is mainly made of proteins and lipids. It controls the movement of substances into and out of the cell.

The **cell wall supports** the cell. It's made of a polymer called **peptidoglycan** (don't worry — you don't need to know what that is).

The **DNA** of a bacterium floats free in the cytoplasm. Most of the DNA is in one long coiled-up strand called the **bacterial chromosome**.

Plasmids are **small loops of DNA** that aren't part of the chromosome. Plasmids contain genes for things like **antibiotic resistance**, and can be passed between bacteria. Plasmids are **not always** present in bacteria.

Some bacteria also have a **capsule** made up of secreted **slime**. It helps to **protect** the bacteria from attack by cells of the immune system (see p. 32).

Some Bacteria Cause Disease by Damaging Cells Directly

Bacteria can cause **physical damage** to cells in many ways:

1)   Some rupture host cells to **release the nutrients** (proteins, fats etc.) inside them.

2)   Once inside a host cell, some **break down** nutrients for their own use. This starves and eventually **kills** the **host cell**.

3)   Some **replicate** inside a host cell then **burst** the cell to get out.

The cell the bacteria have invaded and are reproducing inside is called the host cell.

One example of a disease caused by a bacterium damaging **host cells** is tuberculosis:

Tuberculosis (TB)

- **Tuberculosis is a lung disease** caused by the bacterium *Mycobacterium tuberculosis*.

- TB spreads by 'droplet infection' — infected people cough out droplets of water or mucus into the **air** that contain the bacteria, which are then **breathed** in by other people. The bacteria invade a type of white blood cell found in the lungs, where they can lay **dormant** for many years.

- When the host's immune system becomes **weakened**, e.g. by old age, they replicate **inside** the cells and spread to other tissues, causing **damage** to the affected tissues.

- **Symptoms** include **weight loss** and **coughing**.

- TB can be **prevented** with the **BCG vaccine** and **treated** using **antibiotics**, but there's a big problem with **antibiotic-resistant** strains.

Bacteria

Some **Bacteria** Produce **Toxins** That Can Cause **Disease**

Most kinds of bacteria that infect humans produce **damaging chemicals** called **toxins**. Toxins can cause disease by:

1) **Damaging** the cell structure, e.g. by puncturing the cell membrane or breaking down proteins.
2) **Inhibiting metabolic processes** (reactions in cells and the body that we need to stay alive).
3) Over-stimulating the immune system.

Salmonella bacteria are a good example of bacteria that cause disease by producing toxins:

Tarquin's chicken looked a bit peaky but he wasn't convinced it had *Salmonella*.

Salmonella

- Raw and undercooked food (especially poultry) can sometimes contain *Salmonella* bacteria, which cause **food poisoning**.
- If you eat contaminated food the bacteria infect the **gut epithelial cells**, where they **divide** and produce **toxins** that prevent absorption of water from the large intestine. This causes **diarrhoea**.
- Other **symptoms** include **stomach ache**, **vomiting**, **inflammation** and **fever**.
- Infection can be **avoided** by **thoroughly cooking food** to kill the bacteria. It's also important to make sure that frozen meat is properly **thawed** before cooking.
- Sufferers should have plenty to **drink** and lots of **rest**. Sometimes **antibiotics** are needed to help speed up recovery.

Antibiotics Inhibit **Bacterial Metabolism**

Antibiotics kill bacteria (or inhibit their growth) because they **interfere** with metabolic reactions that are **crucial** for the growth and life of the cell.

1) Some **inhibit enzymes** that are needed to make the chemical **bonds** in bacterial **cell walls**. This prevents the bacteria from **growing** properly. It can also lead to **cell death** — the weakened cell wall can't take the **pressure** as water moves into the cell by **osmosis**. This can cause the cell to **burst**.
2) Some **inhibit protein production** by binding to bacterial **ribosomes**. All **enzymes** are proteins, so if the cell can't make proteins, it can't make enzymes. This means it can't carry out important **metabolic processes** that are needed for growth and development.

Practice Questions

Q1   What is the function of a bacterial flagellum?

Q2   Name the two organelles in bacteria that contain DNA.

Q3   Describe two ways that toxins can cause disease.

Q4   Name two processes in a bacterial cell that antibiotics can inhibit.

Exam Questions

Q1   Describe the cause, symptoms and control of tuberculosis.   [3 marks]

Q2   Describe how antibiotics that inhibit ribosomes inhibit bacterial growth.   [4 marks]

Diarrhoea is hereditary — it runs in your jeans...

Not a happy couple of pages — slime, food poisoning, diarrhoea... eugh. Unfortunately you need to learn it all — the structure of a prokaryotic cell, the cause, symptoms and control of TB and Salmonella... oh, and how antibiotics work...

Evaluating Resistance Data

Another evaluating data page. You could be quizzed on study data in your exam, and here at CGP we like to make sure you're good and ready for anything those pesky examiners could throw at you.

Overuse of Antibiotics can Increase Antibiotic Resistance in Bacteria

Some populations of bacteria have evolved **antibiotic resistance** — certain antibiotics no longer affect them. E.g. **MRSA** (methicillin-resistant *Staphylococcus aureus*) is a strain of bacteria that's **unaffected** by the antibiotic methicillin. It's generally accepted that the **overuse** of antibiotics **increases the rate** at which populations of bacteria develop antibiotic resistance. In your exam, you could be asked to **evaluate the evidence** for the links between antibiotic use and antibiotic resistance.

Here's some evidence to get your teeth into:

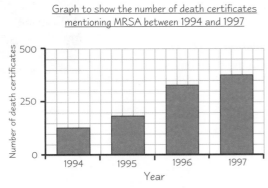

Graph to show the number of death certificates mentioning MRSA between 1994 and 1997

Study 1 — MRSA on death certificates

This study investigated the **number** of death certificates **mentioning** MRSA in the UK between 1994 and 1997. The data was collected from **UK death certificates** issued between these dates.

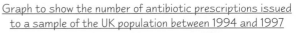

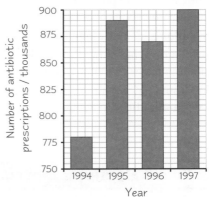

Graph to show the number of antibiotic prescriptions issued to a sample of the UK population between 1994 and 1997

Study 2 — Antibiotic prescriptions

This study **counted** the number of antibiotic prescriptions given out from 1994 to 1997. The information was gathered from a **sample population** covering 211 practices across the UK, which look after **1.4 million** people.

Here are some of the things you might be asked to do:

1) **Describe the data** — **Study 1** shows that the number of death certificates mentioning MRSA **increased** between 1994 and 1997. **Study 2** shows that generally the number of antibiotic prescriptions given **increased** between 1994 and 1997.

2) **Draw conclusions** — If you're given **two graphs** you might be asked to see what conclusions you can draw using the graphs **combined**. These graphs show that the **increase** in the number of antibiotic prescriptions shows a **positive correlation** with an **increase** in the number of death certificates mentioning MRSA.

3) **Check the evidence backs up any conclusions** — E.g. Dr Bottril said, 'This data **proves** that the increase in antibiotic prescriptions **caused** an increase in antibiotic resistance'. Does the data support this conclusion? No, there's a **link** between the number of prescriptions and MRSA being **mentioned** on death certificates, but **that's all**. Also, study 1 only looked at MRSA — not **all forms** of antibiotic resistance.

4) **Evaluate the methodology** — For example:
   - The **time period** is relatively **short** — only 4 years. This trend may not continue, e.g. data for the next four years may show prescriptions rising further whilst resistant bacteria levels fall.
   - The number of death certificates mentioning MRSA **increased** but this doesn't necessarily mean the number of MRSA **infections** increased. The number of MRSA infections each year may have **stayed the same**, showing no increasing trend (just more people are dying from MRSA or the method for **identifying** and reporting MRSA has improved).
   - Study 2 includes all forms of **antibiotic** — prescriptions for **methicillin** may not have increased.

Because of **evidence** like this, scientists are relatively confident that increased antibiotic usage is **linked** to rising levels of antibiotic resistance. **Decision makers** have used this **scientific knowledge** to set **guidelines** on the appropriate use of antibiotics.

Evaluating Resistance Data

Antibiotic Resistance can be Tested Experimentally

There are lots of reasons why you might want to test bacteria for antibiotic resistance.
E.g. doctors need to find out **which** antibiotics will **treat** a **patient's infection**. Here's one way to do it:

1) The bacteria to be tested are **spread** onto an agar plate.

2) Paper discs **soaked** with antibiotics are placed apart on the plate.
   Various **concentrations** of antibiotics should be used.

3) The plate is **incubated** to allow the bacteria to grow (forming a **lawn**).
   Anywhere the bacteria **can't grow** can be seen as a **clear patch** in the
   lawn of bacteria. This is called an **inhibition zone**.

4) The size of an **inhibition zone** tells you how well an antibiotic works.
   The **larger** the zone, the **more** the bacteria were inhibited from growing.

It's important to perform the whole experiment using aseptic techniques (sterile conditions), to make sure only the type of bacteria you want to test grows.

Evaluate the data, conclusions and methodology:

1) <u>Describe the data</u> — An **inhibition zone** can be seen
   around the 125 mg and 250 mg doses of methicillin
   and the 250 mg dose of streptomycin. **No zone** is
   observed for the 125 mg dose of streptomycin or
   either dose of tetracycline.

2) <u>Draw conclusions</u> — This time be **precise** about
   what the data shows. The bacteria are **inhibited** by
   125 mg of **methicillin** and **250 mg** of **streptomycin**,
   but are **resistant** to at least **250 mg** of **tetracycline**.

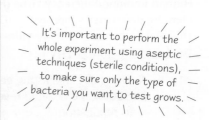

3) <u>Check the evidence backs up any conclusions</u> —
   Dr Ellingham decided that this bacterium can **only** be
   treated with repeated 250 mg doses of **streptomycin**. The evidence **doesn't** back up this conclusion.
   This experiment only tested a **single dose** — repeated 125 mg doses of streptomycin may have **inhibited** growth.
   The increase from 125 mg to 250 mg is quite **large** — a 150 mg dose of streptomycin may also have worked.
   Methicillin also **inhibited** the bacteria so could be used to treat this infection.

4) <u>Evaluate the methodology</u> — **Smaller increments** between measurements would **increase the precision** of the
   results. In this experiment they used a control, which increases reliability. The **negative control** is a disc soaked
   in sterile water. The bacteria grew around this disc, which shows the paper disc **alone** doesn't kill the bacteria.

Practice Questions

Q1 State one factor that might be increasing the rate at which bacteria evolve resistance to antibiotics?

Q2 What does a clear zone around an antibiotic-soaked disc suggest?

Q3 How can you increase the precision of a result?

Exam Question

Q1 The graph on the right shows the results from a study that counted the
   number of death certificates that mentioned *Staphylococcus aureus* or
   methicillin-resistant *S. aureus* (MRSA) in the UK between 1998 and 2002.

   a) Describe what the graph shows. [2 marks]

   b) Evaluate the methodology of the study. [2 marks]

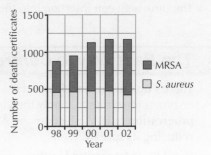

R-E-S-I-S-T-A-N-T — find out what it means to me...

The example above is testing the resistance of a bacterium to various antibiotics. You could be given data to interpret about the antibiotic action of an unknown substance. Don't worry though — the experiment methodology would be fairly similar.

Viruses

Viruses aren't cells like bacteria. They're not even living things — they can only reproduce inside the cells of another organism (called the host). All viruses cause disease, and you need to know all about one particularly nasty blighter...

HIV is the Virus That Causes AIDS

Human immunodeficiency virus (HIV) infects immune system cells (see page 32). It eventually leads to **acquired immune deficiency syndrome (AIDS)**. AIDS is a condition where the immune system **deteriorates** and eventually **fails**. This makes the sufferer more **vulnerable** to **other infections**, like pneumonia (see next page).

The basic structure of **HIV** is:

1) A **core** that contains the **genetic material** (RNA) and some **proteins** (including the enzyme **reverse transcriptase**, which is needed for virus replication).

2) An **outer coating** of protein called a **capsid**.

3) An **extra outer layer** called an **envelope**. This is made of **membrane** stolen from the cell membrane of a previous host cell.

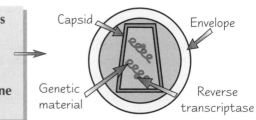

HIV Replicates Inside Its Host's Cells

HIV (and all other viruses) can only **reproduce** inside the cells of the organism it has infected. It doesn't have the equipment (such as **enzymes** and **ribosomes**) to replicate on its own, so it uses those of the **host cell**.

Here's how HIV replicates:

1) The envelope **attaches** to a **receptor** molecule on the cell membrane of the host cell.

2) The capsid is released into the cell, where it **uncoats** and releases the **genetic material** (RNA) into the cell's cytoplasm.

3) Inside the cell, reverse transcriptase is used to make a **complementary** strand of DNA from the **viral RNA template** (see p. 46 for more on DNA and RNA).

4) From this, **double-stranded DNA** is made and **inserted** into the human DNA.

5) Host cell enzymes are used to make **viral proteins** from the **viral DNA** found within the human DNA.

6) The viral proteins are **assembled** into **new viruses**, which **bud** from the cell and go on to infect other cells.

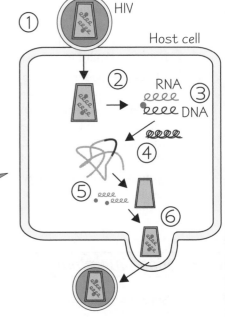

The time between insertion into the human genome and replication can vary and is known as the **latency period**.

The Best Way to Control HIV is to Reduce Its Spread

There's **no cure** or **vaccine** for HIV. **Antiviral** drugs can be used to treat HIV. They work by inhibiting virus-specific enzymes (enzymes that **only** the virus uses), like reverse transcriptase. But these treatments can only **slow down** the **progression** of HIV infection and AIDS. Because you can't kill HIV with **drugs**, the best way to control it is by **reducing its spread**.

HIV is **transmitted** in **three** main ways:

1) Via unprotected **sexual intercourse**.

2) Through **infected bodily fluids** (like blood), e.g. **blood transfusions, sharing needles**.

3) From **mother** to **fetus** (through the placenta, breast milk or during childbirth).

So, the spread of HIV can be **controlled** by:

1) **Using barrier contraceptives**, e.g. condoms.

2) **Screening** blood donor volunteers.

3) Not sharing **hypodermic needles**.

4) Taking **antiviral drugs** during pregnancy.

Viruses

People with **AIDS** Suffer from a Range of **Illnesses**

People with HIV are classed as having AIDS when **symptoms** of their **failing immune system** start to **appear**. AIDS sufferers generally develop diseases that **wouldn't** cause serious problems in people with a **healthy** immune system. The length of time between **infection** with HIV and the **development** of AIDS **varies** between individuals but it's usually **8-10 years**.

1) The **initial symptoms** of AIDS include **minor infections** of mucous membranes (e.g. the inside of the nose, ears and genitals), and recurring respiratory infections.

2) As AIDS **progresses** the number of **immune system cells decreases** further. Patients become susceptible to **more serious infections** including chronic diarrhoea, severe bacterial infections and tuberculosis.

3) During the **late stages** of AIDS patients have a very **low number** of immune system cells and suffer from a **range of serious infections** such as toxoplasmosis of the brain (a parasite infection) and candidiasis of the respiratory system (fungal infection). It's these serious infections that kill AIDS patients, not HIV itself.

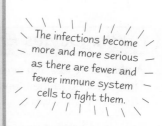
The infections become more and more serious as there are fewer and fewer immune system cells to fight them.

The length of time that people survive with AIDS varies a lot (from **2 weeks to 20 years**), but the average survival time is about **9 months**. Factors that affect survival time include **existing infections**, the **strain of HIV** they're infected with, **fitness level**, **age** and access to **healthcare**.

Antibiotics **Don't Work** Against **Viruses**

1) Antibiotics kill **bacteria** by **interfering** with their metabolic reactions. They target the **bacterial enzymes** and **ribosomes** used in these reactions (see page 27).

2) Bacterial enzymes and ribosomes are **different** from **human** enzymes and ribosomes. Antibiotics are designed to **only target** the bacterial ones so they don't damage human cells. Makes sense.

3) Viruses **don't have their own** enzymes and ribosomes — they use the ones in the host's cells. So because human viruses use human enzymes and ribosomes to replicate, antibiotics **can't** inhibit them because they **don't** target human processes.

4) Most **antiviral drugs** are designed to target the few **virus-specific enzymes** (enzymes that only the virus uses) that exist. E.g. HIV uses **reverse transcriptase** to replicate (see p. 30). Human cells **don't** use this enzyme so drugs can be designed to inhibit it **without affecting** the host cell. These drugs are called reverse-transcriptase inhibitors.

Practice Questions

Q1 List three ways that HIV is transmitted and three ways in which it can be controlled.

Q2 Why can't antibiotics be used to treat HIV?

Q3 Describe the six main steps in HIV replication.

Exam Questions

Q1 Describe, using a diagram, the structure of HIV. [5 marks]

Q2 A new antiviral therapy is being designed against integrase, a HIV enzyme that is used by the virus to integrate its genetic material into the host cell's DNA. Explain how this type of drug could disrupt virus replication without affecting the host cell. [4 marks]

Viruses just aren't funny — they can be really dangerous and hard to treat...

Well, apart from rhinoviruses, which cause colds, but they're only funny because of the name. It's actually quite a logical name — rhino comes from the Greek for nose. So they're literally nose viruses. If I was a virus I'd choose somewhere better to infect... Anyway, you need to learn this stuff, so scribble everything down and see what you remember.

The Immune Response

The immune response is our reaction to something foreign in the body, such as a pathogen. Many funny sounding cells (e.g. B-cells, phagocytes) help to keep us free from disease. Panic over.

Foreign Antigens Trigger an Immune Response

Antigens are **molecules** (usually proteins or polysaccharides) found on the **surface** of **cells**. When a pathogen (like a bacterium) invades the body, the antigens on its cell surface are **identified as foreign**, which activates cells in the immune system. There are **four** main stages involved in the immune response:

1 Phagocytes Engulf Pathogens

A **phagocyte** (e.g. a macrophage) is a type of **white blood cell** that carries out **phagocytosis** (engulfment of pathogens). They're found in the **blood** and in **tissues** and are the first cells to respond to a pathogen inside the body. Here's how they work:

1) The phagocyte **recognises** the **antigens** on a pathogen.

2) The cytoplasm of the phagocyte moves round the pathogen, **engulfing** it.

3) The pathogen is now contained in a **phagocytic vacuole** (a bubble) in the cytoplasm of the phagocyte.

4) A **lysosome** (an organelle that contains **digestive enzymes**) **fuses** with the phagocytic vacuole. The enzymes **break down** the pathogen.

5) The phagocyte then **presents** the pathogen's antigens. It sticks the antigens on its **surface** to **activate** other immune system cells.

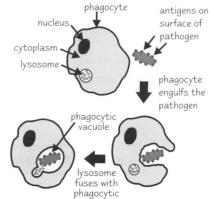

2 Phagocytes Activate T-cells

A **T-cell** is another type of **white blood cell**. It has **proteins** on its surface that **bind** to the **antigens** presented to it by **phagocytes**. This **activates** the T-cell. Different types of T-cells respond in different ways:

1) Some **release substances** to **activate B-cells**.

2) Some **attach** to antigens on a pathogen and **kill** the cell.

3 T-cells Activate B-cells, Which Divide into Plasma Cells

B-cells are also a type of **white blood cell**. They're covered with **antibodies** — proteins that **bind antigens** to form an **antigen-antibody complex**. Each B-cell has a **different shaped antibody** on its membrane, so different ones bind to **different shaped antigens**.

1) When the antibody on the surface of a B-cell meets a **complementary shaped** antigen, it binds to it.

2) This, together with substances released from T-cells, **activates** the B-cell.

3) The activated B-cell **divides**, by mitosis, into **plasma cells**.

4 Plasma Cells Make More Antibodies to a Specific Antigen

Plasma cells are **identical** to the B-cell (they're **clones**). They secrete loads of the **antibody** specific to the antigen. Antibody **functions** include:

1) Coating the pathogen to make it easier for a **phagocyte** to engulf it.

2) Coating the pathogen to **prevent** it from **entering** host cells.

3) **Binding to** and **neutralising** (inactivating) **toxins** produced by the pathogen.

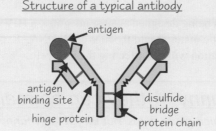

Structure of a typical antibody

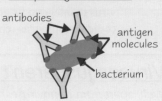

Antibodies bind to antigens on a pathogen's surface

The Immune Response

The **Immune Response** for Antigens can be **Memorised**

The Primary Response

Neil's primary response — to his parents.

1) When an antigen enters the body for the **first time** it activates the immune system. This is called the primary response.

2) The primary response is **slow** because there aren't many B-cells that can make the antibody needed to bind to it.

3) Eventually the body will produce enough of the right antibody to overcome the infection. Meanwhile the infected person will show **symptoms** of the disease.

4) After being exposed to an antigen, both T- and B-cells produce **memory cells**. These memory cells **remain in the body** for a **long** time. Memory T-cells remember the **specific antigen** and will recognise it a second time round. Memory B-cells record the specific **antibodies** needed to bind the antigen.

5) The person is now **immune** — their immune system has the **ability** to respond **quickly** to a 2nd infection.

The Secondary Response

1) If the **same pathogen** enters the body again, the immune system will produce a **quicker**, **stronger** immune response — the **secondary response**.

2) Memory B-cells divide into **plasma cells** that produce the right antibody to the antigen. Memory T-cells divide into the **correct type of T-cells** to kill the cell carrying the antigen.

3) The secondary response often gets rid of the pathogen **before** you begin to show any **symptoms**.

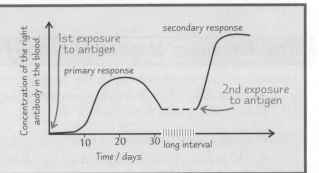

Immunity can be **Passive** or **Active**

1) **Passive immunity** is where you become immune by receiving antibodies made by **another organism**. This can be **natural**, e.g. when antibodies pass from mum to baby through the **placenta** and via **breast milk** (lactation). It can also be **artificial**, e.g. if you've cut yourself on a rusty nail and are worried about tetanus, you can be injected with antibodies against the bacterium that causes it. **Memory cells aren't produced** in passive immunity, so it's only **short-term** protection. But it's **immediate**, unlike active immunity where the primary immune response takes a while (see below).

2) **Active immunity** is where the immune system makes **antibodies of its own** after being stimulated by an **antigen**. This can happen **naturally** when you catch a disease and it causes an immune response. Or it can happen **artificially** when you get a vaccination containing a harmless dose of the **antigen**. Active immunity involves producing **memory cells** to cause a rapid **secondary response** to pathogens.

Practice Questions

Q1 What are antigens?
Q2 What is phagocytosis?
Q3 What are the functions of T-cells and B-cells?

Exam Questions

Q1 Emily had chickenpox as a child. She was exposed to the virus that causes it as a teenager but did not experience any symptoms. Explain why. [10 marks]

Q2 Describe the function of antibodies. [3 marks]

This is getting scary — there's a battle being fought in my own nose...

The last section talked about how HIV causes the immune system to fail. This is because the HIV virus replicates in T-cells. Without T-cells, the pathogen can't be killed by them and B-cells can't be activated. B- and T-cells are also called B- and T-lymphocytes... because scientists seem to enjoy using a long word when a short one will do.

Vaccines

Vaccines are a way of getting immunity without suffering from the infection first time round.
Quite handy if you're going on holiday to an exotic place... well, I can dream...

Vaccines *Give Us* Immunity *Against Some Diseases*

While your B-cells are busy dividing to build up their numbers to deal with a pathogen (i.e. the primary response), you suffer from the disease (see p. 32). **Vaccination** can help avoid this. Vaccines **contain antigens** that cause your body to produce memory cells against a particular pathogen, **without** the pathogen **causing disease**. This means you get the **immunity** without getting any **symptoms**... genius. Vaccines normally contain one of three things:

1) **Dead microorganisms**. The pathogen is **killed** but the antigens remain on its surface, so the immune system responds to the pathogen, without it causing any damage.

2) **Attenuated microorganisms**. Some strains of a pathogen stimulate the **immune system**, but they don't actually cause the disease because they've been **weakened** in the lab.

3) **Isolated antigens**. Sometimes the antigen can be **separated** from the pathogen and injected to trigger an immune response.

The Benefits *of* Mass Vaccination Programmes *Outweigh the* Risks

Mass vaccination programmes are where large numbers of people are vaccinated at once. They're usually funded by a large organisation, like a government or charity. E.g. the UK government funds an immunisation programme for all UK children, which starts at two months old.

There are **two** main **benefits** of vaccination:

1) The person vaccinated will **not** get that **disease**... a pretty obvious benefit. They **avoid suffering** from an unpleasant illness and any risk of **permanent effects** from the disease.

2) It creates **herd immunity** — if most people in a **community** are **vaccinated**, the disease becomes extremely **rare**. This means that even people who haven't been vaccinated are **unlikely** to get the disease, because there's no one to catch it from.

Paul couldn't understand why his herd immunity wasn't working...

There is **one** main **risk** of vaccination:
The vaccine may cause **side effects** such as a runny nose, slight rash etc. In some cases the side effects can be **serious**, although this is very **rare**. For example, the **polio vaccine** can produce a severe **allergic reaction** in some people, causing **breathing difficulties**, **dizziness** and **fever**. However, there's less than **one in a million** chance of getting this kind of reaction from taking the polio vaccine.

New Evidence *About* Vaccines *is* Questioned *by* Scientists

When a **study** presents evidence for a **new theory** (e.g. that a vaccine has a dangerous side effect) it's important that other scientists come up with **more evidence** in order to **validate** (confirm) the theory. To validate the theory other scientists may **repeat** the study and try to **reproduce** the results, or **conduct other studies** to try to prove the same theory.

EXAMPLE

- In 1998, a study was published about the **safety** of the **measles**, **mumps** and **rubella** (MMR) **vaccine**. The study was based on **12 children** with **autism** (a life-long developmental disability).
- This study concluded that there may be a **link** between the MMR vaccine and autism.

Not everyone was convinced by this study though because:

- The study had a **very small sample size** of only 12 children, which decreases its reliability, as there's an increased likelihood of the results being due to **chance**.
- The study may have been **biased**. One of the scientists was helping some parents of autistic children gain scientific evidence for a **lawsuit** against the MMR vaccine manufacturer.

Vaccines

Conflicting Evidence Leads to Further Scientific Investigation

Studies carried out by other scientists **contradicted** the finding of the 1998 study — they didn't find any link.
So there have been **further scientific studies** to try to sort out the **conflicting** evidence.

EXAMPLE continued...

In **2005**, a **Japanese** study was published about the incidence of autism in an area of Japan.
They looked at the medical records of **30 000 children** born in Yokohama between **1988 and 1996**. The study counted the number of children that developed **autism** before the age of seven. The **MMR jab** was first **introduced in Japan in 1989** and was **stopped in 1993**. During this time the MMR vaccine was administered to children at **12 months old**.
The graph shows the results of the study.

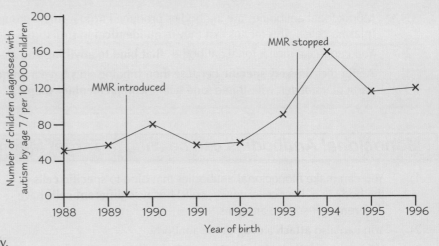

In the exam you could be asked to **evaluate evidence** like this. Don't worry though — it's fairly easy.

1) You might be asked to **explain the data...**
   The graph shows that the number of children diagnosed with autism continued to **rise** after the MMR vaccine was **stopped**. E.g. from all the children born in 1992, who did receive the MMR jab, about 60 out of 10 000 were diagnosed with autism before the age of seven. However, from all the children born in 1994, who did not receive the MMR jab, about 160 out of 10 000 of them were diagnosed with autism before the age of seven.

2) ...or **draw conclusions**
   There is **no link** between the MMR vaccine and autism.

3) ... or **evaluate the methodology**
   You can be much more confident in this study, compared to the 1998 study, because the **sample size** was so **large** — 30 000 children were studied. A larger sample size means that the results are less likely to be due to **chance**.

Practice Questions

Q1 How do vaccines cause immunity?

Q2 What are the benefits of mass vaccination programmes?

Q3 What is the main risk of vaccination?

Exam Question

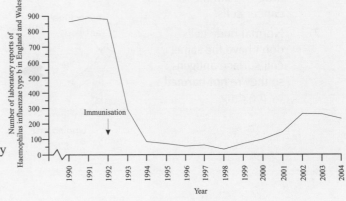

Q1 The graph on the right shows the number of laboratory reports of *Haemophilus influenzae* type b (Hib), in England and Wales, from 1990 to 2004. Hib affects children and can lead to meningitis and pneumonia.

a) Why did the number of cases of Hib decrease after 1992? [2 marks]
b) Due to a shortage of the normal vaccine in 2000-2001, a different type of Hib vaccine was used. What effect did this have on the number of cases of Hib? [1 mark]
c) The Hib vaccine is an isolated antigen vaccine. What two other types of vaccine are there? [2 marks]

An injection of dead bugs — roll on my next vaccine...

After the 1998 study, some parents were worried about giving their kids the MMR vaccine, so the number of children given the vaccine fell. With fewer children in each community protected by the vaccine, herd immunity decreased. This meant that more people were vulnerable to the diseases, so the number of cases of measles, mumps and rubella went up.

Antibodies in Medicine

Antibodies aren't only used by the immune system — they're also used by doctors as delivery boys (for drugs) and medical detectives (to diagnose conditions). Poirot eat your heart out.

Monoclonal Antibodies can be used to Target Specific Substances or Cells

1) Monoclonal antibodies are antibodies produced from a single group of genetically identical B-cells (plasma cells). This means that they're all **identical** in structure.

2) You can make monoclonal antibodies **that bind to anything** you want, e.g. a cell antigen or other substance.

3) Antibodies are **very specific** because their binding sites have a **unique tertiary structure** that only a particular antigen will fit into (one with a **complementary shape**).

Monoclonal Antibodies can be used to Target Medication

1) You can make monoclonal antibodies that bind to **specific cells** in the body (e.g. liver cells, cancer cells) because **different cells** have **different** cell-surface **antigens**.

2) You can also **attach** a **drug** to the antibody.

3) When this antibody-drug is given to the patient, it will only accumulate in the body where you want it to.

4) So, the **side effects** of the drug are reduced because it only affects specific cells.

Peggy Sue was determined to prove that she could be just as accurate as an antibody...

EXAMPLE

Monoclonal antibodies can be used to target **anti-cancer drugs** to **cancer cells**:

1) Cancer cells have **antigens** on their **plasma membranes** that **aren't** found on normal body cells. They're called **tumour markers**.

2) In the lab, **monoclonal antibodies** are made that will bind to the tumour markers.

3) An **anti-cancer drug** is attached to the antibodies.

4) The antibodies are **administered** to a cancer patient.

5) When the antibodies come into **contact** with the cancer cells they will **bind** to the tumour markers, via their **antigen binding sites** (see p. 32).

6) The anti-cancer drug will **kill** the cancer cells.

7) Normal body cells don't have the same cell-surface antigens, so they're **not harmed** by the drug.

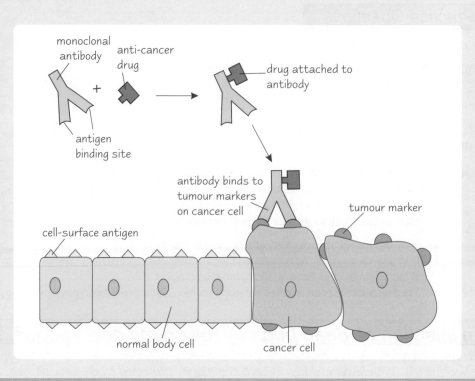

Antibodies in Medicine

Monoclonal Antibodies can be used in Medical Diagnosis

Pregnancy tests are a good example of how monoclonal antibodies can be used in medical diagnosis. The substance being detected in pregnancy tests is a hormone called **human chorionic gonadotropin (hCG)**. It's produced by cells of the placenta and embryo, and ends up in the mother's urine, so it's a good indication of a pregnancy. Here's how it works:

① The application area (the bit of the stick you wee on) contains **antibodies for hCG** that are attached to a **coloured bead** (**blue**). The test strip contains more **antibodies for hCG** that are stuck in place (**immobilised**) — but these ones don't have beads attached.

② When urine is applied to the application area any hCG will **bind** to the antibody on the beads, forming an **antibody-antigen complex**.

③ The urine **moves** up the stick to the **test strip**, **carrying** any **beads** with it.

If there **is hCG present** the **test strip turns blue** because the **immobilised** antibody binds to any hCG — concentrating the hCG-antibody complex with the **blue beads** attached.

If **no hCG** is present, the beads will **pass through** the test area **without** binding to anything, and so it **won't** go blue.

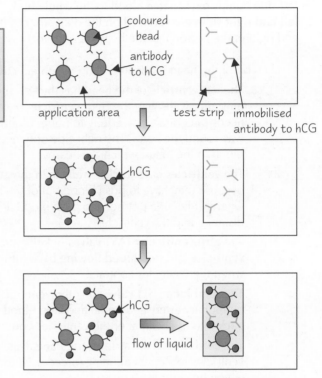

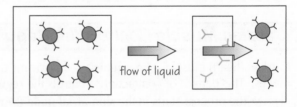

Practice Questions

Q1 What are monoclonal antibodies?

Q2 What do monoclonal antibodies recognise on the surface of cells?

Q3 Give one advantage of using monoclonal antibodies to target medication.

Q4 What three things are present on the sensitive pad of a pregnancy test kit?

Exam Questions

Q1 A pregnancy test is specific for the hormone human chorionic gonadotropin. Explain why. [4 marks]

Q2 Describe how monoclonal antibodies can be used to target a drug to cancer cells. [4 marks]

Monoclonal antibodies — sound like monsters out of Dr. Who to me...

Using antibodies to target drugs is at the forefront of science. As scientists find more cancer-specific antigens, more monoclonal antibodies can be developed, to target drugs to more types of cancer. So antibodies are pretty useful really. I wonder if they've made antibodies to target fat cells... that'd clear up my cellulite a treat...

The Heart

To understand cardiovascular disease first you need to know about how the heart works normally...

The **Heart** Consists of **Two Muscular Pumps**

The diagram on the right shows the **internal structure** of the heart. The **right side** pumps **deoxygenated blood** to the **lungs** and the **left side** pumps **oxygenated blood** to the **whole body**. Note — the **left and right sides** are **reversed** on the diagram, cos it's the left and right of the person that the heart belongs to.

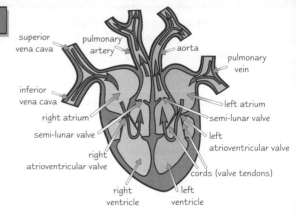

Each bit of the heart is adapted to do its job effectively.

1) The **left ventricle** of the heart has **thicker**, more muscular walls than the **right ventricle**, because it needs to contract powerfully to pump blood all the way round the body. The right side only needs to get blood to the lungs, which are nearby.

2) The **ventricles** have **thicker walls** than the **atria**, because they have to push blood out of the heart whereas the atria just need to push blood a short distance into the ventricles.

3) The **atrioventricular (AV) valves** link the atria to the ventricles and **stop blood flowing back** into the atria when the ventricles contract.

4) The **semi-lunar (SL) valves** link the ventricles to the pulmonary artery and aorta, and **stop blood flowing back** into the heart after the ventricles contract.

5) The **cords** attach the atrioventricular valves to the ventricles to stop them being forced up into the atria when the ventricles contract.

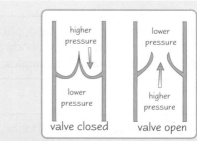

The **valves** only open one way — whether they're open or closed depends on the relative **pressure** of the heart chambers. If there's higher pressure **behind** a valve, it's forced **open**, but if pressure is higher **in front** of the valve it's forced **shut**.

Cardiac Muscle Controls the **Regular Beating** of the Heart

Cardiac (heart) muscle is '**myogenic**' — this means that it can contract and relax without receiving signals from nerves. This pattern of contractions controls the **regular heartbeat**.

1) The process starts in the **sino-atrial node (SAN)**, which is in the wall of the **right atrium**.

2) The SAN is like a pacemaker — it sets the **rhythm** of the heartbeat by sending out regular **waves of electrical activity** to the atrial walls.

3) This causes the right and left **atria** to **contract at the same time**.

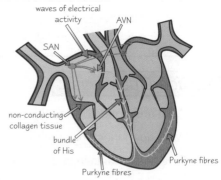

4) A band of non-conducting **collagen tissue** prevents the waves of electrical activity from being passed directly from the atria to the ventricles.

5) Instead, these waves of electrical activity are transferred from the SAN to the **atrioventricular node (AVN)**.

6) The AVN is responsible for passing the waves of electrical activity on to the bundle of His. But, there's a **slight delay** before the AVN reacts, to make sure the ventricles contract **after** the atria have emptied.

7) The **bundle of His** is a group of muscle fibres responsible for conducting the waves of electrical activity to the finer muscle fibres in the right and left ventricle walls, called the **Purkyne fibres**.

8) The Purkyne fibres carry the waves of electrical activity into the muscular walls of the right and left ventricles, causing them to **contract simultaneously**, from the bottom up.

Sometimes, **disease** of the heart can cause the mechanisms that control the heatbeat to **fail**. An **artificial pacemaker** can be used to control heartbeat if the **pacemaker cells don't work properly**. It's a device that's implanted under the skin and has a wire going to the heart. It produces an **electric current** to stimulate the heart to beat.

The Heart

The **Cardiac Cycle** Pumps Blood Round the Body

The cardiac cycle is an ongoing sequence of **contraction** and **relaxation** of the atria and ventricles that keeps blood **continuously** circulating round the body. The **volume** of the atria and ventricles **changes** as they contract and relax. **Pressure** changes also occur, due to the changes in chamber volume (e.g. decreasing the volume of a chamber by contraction will increase the pressure of a chamber). The cardiac cycle can be simplified into three stages:

① Ventricles relax, atria contract

The **ventricles are relaxed**. The **atria contract**, decreasing the volume of the chamber and **increasing** the **pressure** inside the chamber. This **pushes** the blood into the ventricles. There's a slight **increase** in **ventricular pressure** and **chamber volume** as the **ventricles receive the ejected blood** from the contracting atria.

② Ventricles contract, atria relax

The **atria relax**. The **ventricles contract** (decreasing their volume), **increasing** their **pressure**. The pressure becomes **higher** in the ventricles than the atria, which forces the **AV valves shut** to prevent back-flow.
The **pressure in the ventricles is also higher than in the aorta and pulmonary artery**, which forces **open** the **SL valves** and blood is forced out into these arteries.

③ Ventricles relax, atria relax

The **ventricles and the atria both relax**. The higher pressure in the pulmonary artery and aorta closes the SL valves to prevent back-flow into the ventricles. Blood returns to the heart and the **atria fill again** due to the higher pressure in the vena cava and pulmonary vein. In turn this starts to **increase** the **pressure** of the atria. As the ventricles continue to **relax**, their **pressure falls below the pressure of the atria** and so the **AV valves open**. This allows blood to flow **passively** (without being pushed by atrial contraction) into the ventricles from the atria. The atria contract, and the whole process begins again.

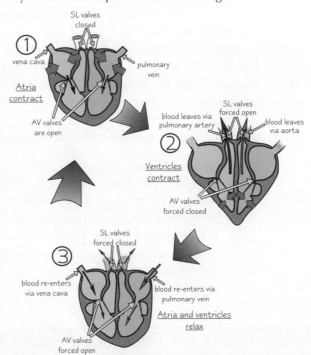

Cardiac contraction is also called systole and relaxation is called diastole.

Practice Questions

Q1 Which side of the heart carries oxygenated blood?

Q2 Why is the left ventricle wall more muscular than the right ventricle wall?

Q3 What does "myogenic" mean?

Q4 Describe the roles of the SAN and the AVN.

Exam Questions

Q1 Describe the pressure changes that occur in the heart during contraction and relaxation. [3 marks]

Q2 Explain how valves in the heart stop blood going back the wrong way. [6 marks]

Learn these pages off by heart...

You don't have to think consciously about making your heart beat — your body does it for you. So you couldn't stop it beating even if for some strange reason you wanted to. Which is nice to know. Anyway, make sure you know all about the structure of the heart, and how the different parts work together to make it beat and pump blood all around the body.

Blood Vessels

The heart, along with various types of blood vessels, make up the circulatory system. Without this system, our cells wouldn't get the substances they need and waste substances wouldn't be removed from them.

Multicellular Organisms Need Mass Transport Systems

1) All cells **need energy** — most cells get energy via **aerobic respiration**.

2) The raw materials for this are **glucose** and **oxygen**, so the body has to make sure it can deliver enough of these to all its cells.

3) In single-celled organisms, these materials can **diffuse directly** into the cell across the cell membrane. The diffusion rate is quick because of the **short distance** the substances have to travel (see p. 20).

4) In **multicellular** organisms (like us), diffusion across the outer membrane would be **too slow** because of the **large distance** the substances would have to travel to reach **all** the cells — think of how far it is from your skin to your heart cells.

5) So, multicellular organisms have **mass transport systems**:

> 1) The **mass transport systems** are used to **carry raw materials** from specialised **exchange organs** (e.g. the lungs and the digestive system) to the body cells and to **remove metabolic waste** (e.g. carbon dioxide).
>
> 2) In mammals, the mass transport system is the **circulatory system**, where **blood** is used to transport substances around the body.
>
> 3) Individual cells in tissues and organs get **nutrients** and **oxygen** from the blood and dispose of **metabolic waste** into the blood.

Richard had a different idea of mass transport from his biology teacher.

Substances are Transported Round the Body in Blood Vessels

You need to know about three types of blood vessel — arteries, veins and capillaries. Read on...

Artery

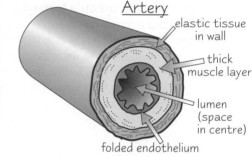

elastic tissue in wall

thick muscle layer

lumen (space in centre)

folded endothelium

> 1) **Arteries** carry blood from the heart **to the rest of the body**. They're thick-walled, muscular and have elastic tissue in the walls to cope with the **high pressure** caused by the heartbeat. The inner lining (**endothelium**) is **folded**, allowing the artery to **expand** — this also helps it to cope with high pressure.

Vein

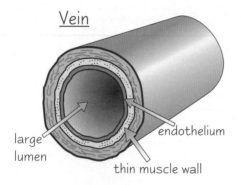

large lumen

endothelium

thin muscle wall

> 2) **Veins** take blood **back to the heart**. They're **wider** than equivalent arteries, with very little elastic or muscle tissue. Veins contain **valves** to stop the blood flowing backwards. Blood flow through the veins is helped by contraction of the **body muscles** surrounding them.

> 3) **Capillaries** are the **smallest** of the blood vessels. They are where **metabolic exchange** occurs — substances are **exchanged** between cells and the capillaries. There are networks of capillaries in tissue (called **capillary beds**), which **increase** the **surface area** for exchange. Capillary walls are only **one cell thick**, which speeds up **diffusion** of substances (e.g. glucose and oxygen) into and out of cells.

Capillary

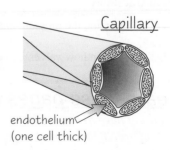

endothelium (one cell thick)

Blood Vessels

Tissue Fluid is Formed from Blood

Tissue fluid is the fluid that **surrounds cells** in tissues. It's made from substances that leave the blood, e.g. oxygen, water and nutrients. Cells take in oxygen and nutrients from the tissue fluid, and release metabolic waste into it. Substances move out of blood capillaries, into the tissue fluid, by **pressure filtration**:

1) At the **start** of the capillary bed, nearest the arteries, the pressure inside the capillaries is **greater** than the pressure in the tissue fluid. This difference in pressure **forces fluid out** of the **capillaries** and into the **spaces** around the cells, forming tissue fluid.

2) As fluid leaves, the pressure reduces in the capillaries — so the pressure is much **lower** at the **end** of the capillary bed that's nearest to the veins.

3) Due to the fluid loss, the **water potential** at the end of the capillaries nearest the veins is **lower** than the water potential in the **tissue fluid** — so some **water re-enters** the capillaries from the tissue fluid at the vein end by **osmosis** (see p. 22 for more on osmosis).

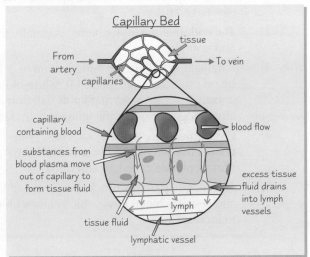

Capillary Bed

Unlike blood, tissue fluid **doesn't** contain **red blood cells** or **big proteins**, because they're **too large** to be pushed out through the capillary walls. Any **excess** tissue fluid is drained into the **lymphatic system**, which transports this excess fluid from the tissues and dumps it back into the circulatory system.

Oedema is a Build-up of Tissue Fluid

Oedema occurs when fluid **isn't drawn back** into the capillaries from the tissues, causing a build-up in the tissues. This excess fluid causes parts of the body (often the legs and ankles) to **swell**. Fluid can also accumulate in the lungs, causing breathlessness. There are two main causes:

1) **High blood pressure** can cause a build-up of tissue fluid. Tissue fluid **formation is increased** as more fluid is pushed out of the capillaries. The high blood pressure makes it **difficult** for water to **move back** into the capillaries, leading to an accumulation in the tissues.

2) **Blockage of lymph vessels** can also cause a build-up of tissue fluid as excess fluid **can't** be **drained** away properly.

Practice Questions

Q1 Why do multicellular organisms need mass transport systems?

Q2 Name three types of blood vessel.

Q3 What is oedema?

Exam Questions

Q1 Explain how tissue fluid is formed and how it is returned to the circulation. [4 marks]

Q2 Explain how the structure of capillaries enables them to carry out metabolic exchange efficiently. [2 marks]

If blood can handle transport this efficiently, the trains have no excuse...

Four hours I was waiting at Preston station this weekend. Four hours! You may have noticed that biologists are obsessed with the relationship between structure and function, so whenever you're learning about the structure of something, make sure you know how this relates to its function. And what better place to start than arteries, veins and capillaries...

Cardiovascular Disease

Cardiovascular diseases affect the heart or blood vessels. There are five you need to know about, so here they are...

Most **Cardiovascular Disease** starts with **Atheroma** Formation

1) The wall of an artery is made up of **several layers** (see page 40).

2) The **endothelium** (inner lining) is usually smooth and unbroken.

3) If **damage** occurs to the endothelium (e.g. by high blood pressure — see page 44), **white blood cells** (mostly macrophages) and **lipids** (fat) from the blood, clump together under the lining to form **fatty streaks**.

4) Over time, more white blood cells, lipids and **connective tissue** build up and harden to form a **fibrous plaque** called an **atheroma**.

5) This plaque **partially blocks** the lumen of the **artery** and **restricts blood flow**, which causes **blood pressure** to **increase**.

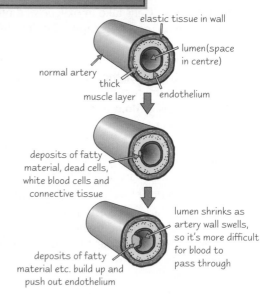

elastic tissue in wall
lumen(space in centre)
normal artery
thick muscle layer
endothelium

deposits of fatty material, dead cells, white blood cells and connective tissue

lumen shrinks as artery wall swells, so it's more difficult for blood to pass through

deposits of fatty material etc. build up and push out endothelium

Atheromas Increase the Risk of Aneurysm, Thrombosis, Angina...

Three types of **cardiovascular disease** that affect the **arteries** are:

Aneurysm — a balloon-like swelling of the artery.

1) Atheroma plaques **damage** and **weaken arteries**. They also **narrow** arteries, **increasing blood pressure**.

2) When **blood** travels through a weakened artery at **high pressure**, it may **push** the **inner layers** of the artery **through the outer elastic layer** to form a **balloon-like swelling** — an **aneurysm**.

3) This aneurysm may **burst**, causing a **haemorrhage** (bleeding).

aneurysm

Thrombosis — formation of a blood clot.

1) An atheroma plaque can **rupture** (burst through) the **endothelium** (inner lining) of an artery.

2) This **damages** the artery wall and leaves a **rough** surface.

3) **Platelets** and **fibrin** (a protein) accumulate at the site of damage and form a **blood clot** (a thrombus).

4) This blood clot can cause a complete **blockage** of the artery, or it can become **dislodged** and block a blood vessel elsewhere in the body.

5) **Debris** from the rupture can cause another blood clot to form further down the artery.

Angina — severe chest pain.

1) The **heart muscle** is supplied with **blood** by the **coronary arteries**.

2) This blood contains the **oxygen** needed by heart muscle cells to carry out **respiration**.

3) The coronary arteries can become **narrowed** due to the formation of **atheromas**.

4) This **reduces** the **blood supply** to parts of the heart muscle.

5) The resulting **decrease in oxygen** causes **heart pain**.

6) Angina is more likely to occur during **exercise**, when the heart needs **more oxygen** because it's working harder.

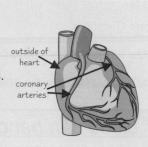

outside of heart
coronary arteries

Cardiovascular Disease

...and *Myocardial Infarction*

1) If a coronary artery becomes **completely blocked** (e.g. by a **blood clot**) an area of the heart muscle will be totally **cut off** from its blood supply, receiving **no oxygen**.

2) This causes a **myocardial infarction** — more commonly known as a **heart attack**.

3) A heart attack can cause **damage** and **death** of the **heart muscle**.

4) **Symptoms** include **pain** in the chest and upper body, **shortness of breath** and **sweating**.

5) If **large areas** of the heart are affected complete **heart failure** can occur, which is often **fatal**.

Treatment *of* Coronary Heart Disease *Includes* Surgery *and* Medication

Coronary heart disease is when the **coronary arteries** have lots of **atheromas** in them, which restricts blood flow to the heart. It's a type of **cardiovascular disease**. **Treatments** include:

1) **Angioplasty.** A deflated **balloon** is inserted into the **narrowed coronary artery** and then **inflated**, which **compresses** the atheroma plaque and **stretches** the artery. This **improves** the **supply of blood** to the **heart muscle** so there's enough **oxygen** for **respiration**.

2) **Coronary by-pass surgery.** This is open-heart surgery, where a bit of a **healthy blood vessel** from another part of the body is used to **bypass** the **narrowed region** of the artery — **improving** the **blood supply**.

3) **Beta-blockers.** These are **drugs** that **lower blood pressure** by reducing the strength of the heartbeat. High blood pressure can cause **damage to arteries** (see p. 44) and **increase** the risk of **atheromas** forming.

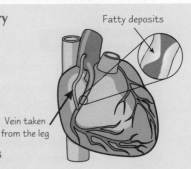

Fatty deposits

Vein taken from the leg

Deep Vein Thrombosis *is Another* Cardiovascular Disease

1) **Deep vein thrombosis (DVT)** is the formation of a **blood clot** in a **vein** deep inside the body — it usually happens in **leg veins**.

2) It can be caused by **prolonged inactivity**, e.g. during **long-haul flights**. Your risk of getting it also **increases** with **age**.

3) The risk of DVT can be reduced by taking **drugs** that **prevent** or **slow blood clotting** (e.g. aspirin), and by wearing **compression stockings** (long socks designed to **support** the leg and **aid circulation**). It's also recommended to **move around** regularly on long-haul flights to increase circulation.

After reading the descriptions in the textbook, Arthur decided that he didn't really want to be a doctor any more.

Practice Questions

Q1 Describe how an atheroma forms.

Q2 List four cardiovascular diseases that atheromas increase the risk of.

Q3 How does coronary by-pass surgery treat coronary heart disease?

Exam Questions

Q1 Describe how atheromas can increase the risk of a person suffering from thrombosis. [2 marks]

Q2 Explain how atheroma formation in the coronary arteries can lead to angina. [4 marks]

Atherosclerosis, aneurysm — more like a spelling test than biology...

There's loads to take in on these pages. You could almost be a doctor by the time you've learnt it all. Well, maybe not — but it'll help you to pass your exam. Anyway, make sure you understand how atheromas form before you do anything else. Once you've got that straight, it'll be much easier to understand the diseases that you need to know about.

Lifestyle and Cardiovascular Disease

As you know, there are treatments for cardiovascular diseases out there, but it's best to try to avoid these diseases in the first place. Because lifestyle plays a large part, it's pretty easy to make preventive changes.

Lifestyle Choices can Affect the Health of Your Heart

In the exam, you might be asked to **evaluate** the evidence for the links between **lifestyle** and **cardiovascular disease**. Factors linked to **lifestyle** that **increase** the **risk** of **cardiovascular disease** include:

1 Poor diet

1) If the **blood cholesterol level** is **high** (above 240 mg per 100 cm³) then the risk of cardiovascular disease is increased.

2) This is because **cholesterol** is one of the main constituents of the **fatty deposits** that form **atheromas** (see p. 42).

3) High blood cholesterol levels are linked to eating **foods high in saturated fat**.

4) A diet **high in salt** also **increases** the **risk** of cardiovascular disease because it increases the risk of **high blood pressure** (see below).

John decided to live on the edge and ordered a fry-up.

2 Cigarette smoking

1) Both **carbon monoxide** and **nicotine**, found in **cigarette smoke**, increase the risk of cardiovascular disease.

2) Carbon monoxide combines with **haemoglobin** and **reduces** the amount of **oxygen transported** in the **blood**, and so reduces the amount of oxygen available to tissues.

3) If heart muscle doesn't receive enough oxygen it can lead to **angina** or a **heart attack** (see previous page).

4) Smoking also **decreases** the **amount** of **antioxidants** in the blood — these are important for **protecting cells** from damage. Fewer antioxidants means **cell damage** in the **coronary artery walls** is more likely, and this can lead to **atheroma formation** (see p. 42).

3 Being overweight or obese

1) People with **excess body fat** are likely to suffer from **high blood pressure** and may have **higher blood cholesterol** levels.

2) Again, this increases the risk of cardiovascular disease.

Other factors include age (risk increases with age) and sex (men are more at risk than women).

4 Physical inactivity

A **lack** of **exercise** increases the risk of cardiovascular disease because it **increases blood pressure**.

5 Excessive alcohol consumption

Drinking too much **alcohol** increases the risk of cardiovascular disease because it also **increases blood pressure**.

Many different lifestyle factors **increase** the risk of cardiovascular disease because they increase the risk of **high blood pressure**:

1) High blood pressure **increases** the **risk** of **damage** to the **artery walls**.

2) Damaged walls have an **increased risk** of **atheroma** formation, causing a further increase in blood pressure.

3) Atheromas can also cause **blood clots** to form (see p. 42).

4) A blood clot could **block flow** of **blood** to the heart, possibly resulting in **myocardial infarction** (see p. 43).

Most of these factors are within our **control** — a person can **choose** to smoke, eat fatty foods, etc. However, some risk factors can't be controlled, such as having a **genetic predisposition** to a cardiovascular disease or having high blood pressure as a result of another **condition**, e.g. some forms of diabetes. Even so, the risk of developing cardiovascular disease can be reduced by removing as many risk factors as you possibly can.

Lifestyle and Cardiovascular Disease

You Might Have to **Evaluate Evidence** of a **Link** Between **Lifestyle** and **Disease**

Take a look at the following example of the sort of study you might see in your exam.

The graph shows the results of a study involving **34 439 male British doctors**. **Questionnaires** were used to find out the smoking habits of the doctors. The number of **deaths** among the participants from ischaemic heart disease (coronary heart disease) was counted, and **adjustments** were made to account for **differences in age**.

Here are some of the things you might be asked to do:

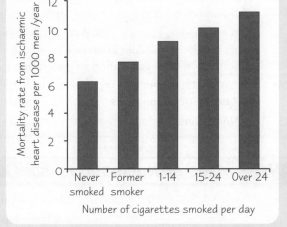

1) <u>Describe the data</u> — The **number** of deaths from ischaemic heart disease **increased** as the number of cigarettes smoked per day **increased**. **Fewer former smokers** and **non-smokers** died of ischaemic heart disease than smokers.

2) <u>Draw conclusions</u> — The graph shows a **positive correlation** between the number of cigarettes smoked per day by **male doctors** and the **mortality rate** from ischaemic heart disease.

3) <u>Check any conclusions are valid</u> — make sure the conclusions **match** the data, e.g. this study only looked at **male doctors** — no females were involved, so you can't say that this trend is true for **everyone**. Also, you couldn't say smoking more cigarettes causes an increased **risk** of heart disease. The data shows **deaths only** and **specifically** from ischaemic heart disease. It could be that the **morbidity rate** (the number who have heart disease) **decreases** with the number of cigarettes a day. But you can't tell that from this data.

4) <u>Comment on the reliability of the results</u> — For example:

See pages 82-84 for more on interpreting data.

   - A **large sample size** was used — 34 439, which **increases** reliability.

   - People (even doctors) can tell **porkies** on questionnaires, **reducing** the **reliability** of results.

   - The study **only** used doctors — this could have swayed the results. Doctor's might be more likely to **avoid** the other risk factors associated with cardiovascular disease (e.g. alcohol, poor diet) and so this might **bias** the data.

   - All the participants have the same job but they **weren't matched** otherwise, e.g. they might not be the same weight, or they might do different amounts of exercise a week, etc. This could have affected the results.

Practice Questions

Q1 How can a diet high in saturated fat contribute to cardiovascular disease?

Q2 How can excessive alcohol consumption increase the risk of cardiovascular disease?

Exam Question

Q1 The results of a study involving 170 000 people in 63 countries have shown a strong correlation between waist measurement and risk of cardiovascular disease. Analysis of the results has shown that waist circumference is independently associated with cardiovascular disease.

   a) Give two reasons why the study provides strong evidence for a link between waist measurement and risk of cardiovascular disease. [2 marks]

   b) Describe how the study must have been conducted in order to show that a high waist measurement is independently associated with cardiovascular disease. [2 marks]

   c) Suggest why waist measurement might be related to risk of cardiovascular disease. [2 marks]

Revision — increasing my risk of headache, stress, boredom...

These evaluating evidence questions come up quite a lot at A level. The examiners like to see that you can analyse the data and that you can pick out the good and bad bits of a study. Luckily, we're giving you plenty of practice at these types of questions. So when you see one lurking in the practice questions, don't be tempted to skip over it — practice makes perfect.

DNA — The Basics

This section's all about our genetic information — the instructions contained within our DNA that are used to build all the proteins in our body. And it's these proteins that make us, well, us — even all the gross bits like snot and pus.

Our **Genetic Material** is **DNA**

1) Your DNA (deoxyribonucleic acid) contains your **genetic information** — that's **all the instructions** needed to **grow and develop** from a fertilised egg to a fully grown adult.

2) The DNA molecules are really **long** and are **coiled** up very tightly, so a lot of genetic information (all that's needed to make you) can fit into a **small space** in the cell nucleus.

3) DNA molecules have a **paired structure** (see below), which makes it much easier to **copy itself**. This is called **self-replication** (see p. 48). It's important for cell division and for passing genetic information from **generation to generation** (see p. 50).

4) DNA contains **genes** — **sections of DNA** that code (contain the instructions) for a specific **sequence of amino acids** that forms a particular **protein**. See next page.

5) RNA (ribonucleic acid) is similar in structure to DNA. It's involved in making **proteins** (see p. 48).

DNA is Made of **Nucleotides** that Contain a **Sugar**, a **Phosphate** and a **Base**

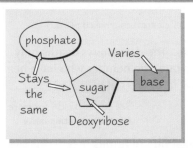

1) DNA is a **polynucleotide** — it's made up of lots of **nucleotides** joined together.

2) Each nucleotide is made from a **pentose sugar** (with 5 carbon atoms), a **phosphate** group and a **nitrogenous base**.

3) The **sugar** in DNA nucleotides is a **deoxyribose** sugar.

4) Each nucleotide has the **same sugar and phosphate**. The **base** on each nucleotide can **vary** though.

5) There are **four** possible bases — adenine (**A**), thymine (**T**), cytosine (**C**) and guanine (**G**).

Two Polynucleotide Strands **Join Together** to Form a **Double-Helix**

1) DNA nucleotides join together to form **polynucleotide strands**.

2) The nucleotides join up between the **phosphate** group of one nucleotide and the **sugar** of another, creating a **sugar-phosphate backbone**.

3) **Two** DNA polynucleotide strands join together by **hydrogen bonding** between the bases.

4) Each base can only join with one particular partner — this is called **specific base pairing**.

5) **Adenine** always pairs with **thymine (A - T)** and **guanine** always pairs with **cytosine (G - C)**.

6) The two strands **wind up** to form the **DNA double-helix**.

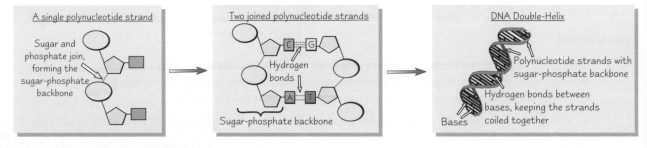

RNA is Very **Similar** to DNA

Like DNA, RNA is made of nucleotides that contain one of four different bases. The nucleotides also form a polynucleotide strand with a sugar-phosphate backbone. But RNA **differs** from DNA in three main ways:

1) The **sugar** in RNA nucleotides is a **ribose sugar** (not deoxyribose).

2) The nucleotides form a **single polynucleotide strand** (not a double one).

3) **Uracil** replaces thymine as a base. Uracil **always pairs** with **adenine** in RNA.

DNA — The Basics

DNA Contains Genes Which Are Instructions for Proteins

1) Proteins are made up of chains of **amino acids**.

2) Each different protein has a **different number** and **order** of amino acids.

3) It's the **order** of **nucleotide bases** in a gene that determines the **order of amino acids** in a particular protein.

4) Each amino acid is coded for by a sequence of **three bases** in a gene.

5) Different sequences of bases code for different amino acids.

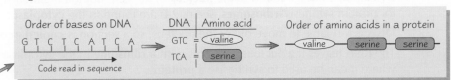

Order of bases on DNA
G T C T C A T C A
Code read in sequence

DNA	Amino acid
GTC	valine
TCA	serine

Order of amino acids in a protein
valine — serine — serine

Genes can Exist in Different Forms Called Alleles

A gene can exist in more than one form. These forms are called **alleles** — the order of bases in each allele is slightly different, so they code for **slightly different versions** of the **same characteristic**. For example, the gene that codes for **blood type** exists as one of three alleles — one codes for type O, another for type A and the other for type B.

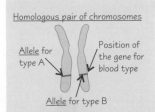

Homologous pair of chromosomes

Allele for type A

Position of the gene for blood type

Allele for type B

Our DNA is stored as **chromosomes** in the nucleus of cells. Humans have **23 pairs** of chromosomes, 46 in total — two number 1's, two number 2's, two number 3's etc. Pairs of matching chromosomes (e.g. the 1's) are called **homologous pairs**. In a homologous pair both chromosomes are the same size and have the **same genes**, although they could have **different alleles**. Alleles coding for the same characteristic are found at the **same position** (**locus**) on each chromosome in a homologous pair.

You can Prove that DNA is the Genetic Material

In the exam you might be asked to **interpret** some evidence that DNA is the genetic material. The experiment below is just one example — so make sure you understand **how** it provides evidence that DNA is the genetic material.

In the 1950s, scientists provided evidence that DNA is the **genetic material** by studying how **viruses** replicate inside bacterial cells. When viruses infect bacteria they **inject** their genetic material into the **cell**. So whatever viral material is found **inside** the bacterial cell must be the genetic material.

1) Scientists labelled the **DNA** of some viruses with radioactive **phosphate**, ^{32}P (**blue**), and the **protein** of some more viruses with radioactive **sulfur**, ^{35}S (**red**).

2) They then let the viruses **infect** some bacteria.

3) When they **separated** the bacteria and viruses they found ^{32}P (**blue**) inside the bacteria and ^{35}S (**red**) on the outside, providing **evidence** that DNA was the **genetic material**.

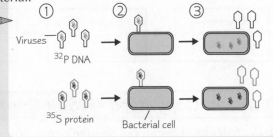

Viruses
^{32}P DNA
^{35}S protein
Bacterial cell

Practice Questions

Q1 What are the three main components of nucleotides?

Q2 What is an allele?

Exam Question

Q1 Describe, using diagrams where appropriate, how nucleotides are joined together in DNA and how two single polynucleotide strands of DNA are joined.

[4 marks]

Give me a D, give me an N, give me an A! What do you get? — very confused...

*You need to know the basic structures of DNA and RNA, and how they differ. Then there's genes to get to grips with. Hmmm, rather you than me, but basically the sequence of **bases** in a gene determines the **order** of amino acids in a protein.*

Protein Synthesis and DNA Replication

Here comes some truly essential stuff — RNA and protein synthesis, enzymes and DNA replication.
I'm afraid it's all horribly complicated — all I can do is keep apologising. Sorry.

DNA is **Copied** into **RNA** for **Protein Synthesis**

1) DNA molecules are found in the **nucleus** of the cell, but the organelles for protein synthesis (**ribosomes**, see p. 24) are found in the **cytoplasm**.

2) DNA is too large to move out of the nucleus, so a section is **copied** into **RNA**.

3) The RNA **leaves** the nucleus and joins with a **ribosome** in the cytoplasm, where it can be used to synthesise a **protein**.

Here's how DNA is copied into RNA:

1) A **single strand** of a gene's DNA is used as a **template**.

2) Free **RNA nucleotides** in the nucleus line up alongside the template strand (**G – C** and **A – U**).

3) **Specific base pairing** means that the RNA ends up being an exact **reverse copy** of the DNA template section (except adenine pairs up with uracil instead of thymine).

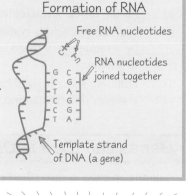

Formation of RNA

Free RNA nucleotides

RNA nucleotides joined together

Template strand of DNA (a gene)

Don't forget that in RNA, adenine pairs up with uracil, not thymine.

Growth and **Development** is **Determined** by **DNA**

1) Enzymes speed up most of our **metabolic pathways** — the **chemical reactions** that occur in the body. These reactions determine how we **grow and develop**.

2) Because enzymes control the metabolic pathways, they **control** our **development**, and ultimately what we look like (our **phenotype**).

3) All enzymes are **proteins**, which are built using the **instructions** contained within genes (see p. 47). The **order of bases** in the gene decides the order of **amino acids** in the protein and so what type of protein (or enzyme) is made.

4) So, our genes help to **determine** our growth, development and **phenotype** because they contain the information to **produce** all our proteins and enzymes.

Ken's bad fashion sense was literally down to his genes. (A genes/jeans joke — classic CGP.)

This flowchart shows how **DNA** controls our **metabolic pathways** and therefore our **phenotype**:

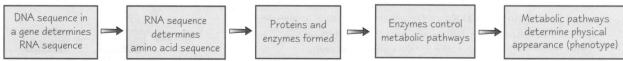

| DNA sequence in a gene determines RNA sequence | RNA sequence determines amino acid sequence | Proteins and enzymes formed | Enzymes control metabolic pathways | Metabolic pathways determine physical appearance (phenotype) |

DNA can **Copy Itself** — **Self-Replication**

DNA copies itself before **cell division** (see p. 50) so that each new cell has the full amount of DNA.

1) The DNA helix **unzips** to form two single strands. Each original single strand acts as a **template** for a new strand.

2) Free-floating nucleotides join to each original template strand by **specific base pairing** — A with T and C with G.

3) The nucleotides on the new strand are **joined** together by the enzyme **DNA polymerase**. **Hydrogen bonds form** between the bases on the original and new strand.

4) Each new DNA molecule contains **one strand** from the **original** DNA molecule sand one **new strand**.

This type of copying is called **semi-conservative replication** because **half** of the new strands of DNA are from the **original** piece of DNA.

Semi-conservative replication

① ②

Hydrogen bonds are broken and the DNA helix unzips.

Bases match up using specific base pairing.

③ New strand

Original DNA strand

DNA polymerase joins the nucleotides. Hydrogen bonds form between the strands.

Protein Synthesis and DNA Replication

You can **Prove** that **Semi-Conservative Replication** Happens

You might have to **interpret** some experimental data that shows DNA replicates semi-conservatively.
Here's one example that uses two **isotopes** of **nitrogen** (DNA contains nitrogen)
— **heavy** nitrogen (^{15}N) and **light** nitrogen (^{14}N).

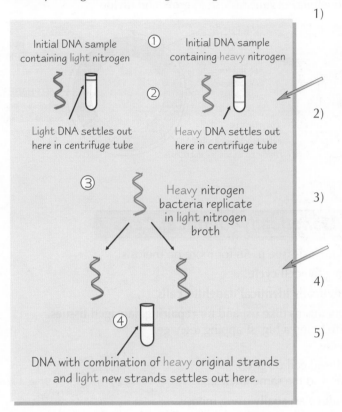

① Initial DNA sample containing light nitrogen
Light DNA settles out here in centrifuge tube

② Initial DNA sample containing heavy nitrogen
Heavy DNA settles out here in centrifuge tube

③ Heavy nitrogen bacteria replicate in light nitrogen broth

④ DNA with combination of heavy original strands and light new strands settles out here.

1) Two samples of bacteria are grown — one in a nutrient broth containing **light** nitrogen, and one in a broth with **heavy** nitrogen. As the **bacteria reproduce**, they **take up nitrogen** from the broth to help make nucleotides for new DNA. So the nitrogen gradually becomes part of the bacteria's DNA.

2) A **sample of DNA** is taken from each batch of bacteria, and spun in a **centrifuge**. The DNA from the **heavy** nitrogen bacteria settles **lower** down the **centrifuge tube** than the DNA from the **light** nitrogen bacteria — because it's **heavier**.

3) Then the bacteria grown in the **heavy** nitrogen broth are **taken out** and put in a broth containing only **light** nitrogen. The bacteria are left for **one round of DNA replication**, and then **another DNA sample** is taken out and spun in the centrifuge.

4) This DNA sample settles out **between** where the **light** nitrogen DNA settled out and where the **heavy** nitrogen DNA settled out.

5) This means that the DNA in the sample contains a **mixture** of **heavy** and **light** nitrogen. The DNA has been **replicated semi-conservatively** in the **light** nitrogen. So the new bacterial DNA molecules contain **one strand** of the **old DNA** containing **heavy** nitrogen and **one strand** of **new DNA** containing **light** nitrogen.

Practice Questions

Q1 Which base pairs up with adenine when making RNA?

Q2 Where is RNA formed?

Q3 What do enzymes do?

Q4 What does phenotype mean?

Q5 Why is DNA copied before cell division?

Q6 What is the function of DNA polymerase in DNA replication?

Exam Questions

Q1 Describe how the DNA of an organism influences its phenotype. [4 marks]

Q2 Describe the semi-conservative method of DNA replication. [7 marks]

What do you get if you cross Tony Blair with Margaret Thatcher?*

DNA self-replication is important — so make sure you understand what's going on. In the exam you could be given unfamiliar data that shows the semi-conservative nature of DNA replication — remember each new DNA molecule is made from one original strand and one new strand. Diagrams are handy for learning stuff like this — so get drawing.

*A semi-conservative.

The Cell Cycle and Mitosis

I don't like cell division. There, I've said it. It's unfair of me, because if it wasn't for cell division I'd still only be one cell big. It's all those diagrams that look like worms nailed to bits of string that put me off.

The **Cell Cycle** is the Process of **Cell Growth** and **Division**

The **cell cycle** is the process that all body cells from **multicellular organisms** use to **grow** and **divide**.

1) The cell cycle **starts** when a cell has been produced by cell division and **ends** with the cell dividing to produce two identical cells.

2) The cell cycle consists of a period of **cell growth** called **interphase** and a period of **cell division** called **mitosis**.

3) Interphase (cell growth) is subdivided into three separate growth stages. These are called G_1, **S** and G_2.

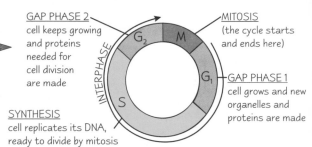

GAP PHASE 2
cell keeps growing and proteins needed for cell division are made

MITOSIS
(the cycle starts and ends here)

GAP PHASE 1
cell grows and new organelles and proteins are made

SYNTHESIS
cell replicates its DNA, ready to divide by mitosis

INTERPHASE

Mitosis is **Cell Division** that Produces **Genetically Identical Cells**

1) There are two types of cell division — **mitosis** and **meiosis** (see p. 56 for more on meiosis).

2) Mitosis is the form of cell division that occurs during the **cell cycle**.

3) In **mitosis** a **parent cell** divides to produce **two genetically identical daughter cells**.

4) Mitosis is needed for the **growth** of multicellular organisms (like us) and for **repairing damaged tissues**. How else do you think you get from being a baby to being a big, strapping teenager — it's because the cells in your body grow and divide.

5) Because we grow (using mitosis) from a **single** fertilised cell (**zygote**), all our body cells contain **exactly the same DNA** and so the **same alleles**.

6) Some organisms (e.g. some plants and fungi) **reproduce asexually** using mitosis.

Alleles are different forms of the same gene. See p. 47 for a recap.

Mitosis has **Four Division Stages**

Mitosis is really one **continuous process**, but it's described as a series of **division stages** — prophase, metaphase, anaphase and telophase. **Interphase** comes **before** mitosis in the cell cycle — it's when cells grow and replicate their DNA ready for division.

Interphase — The cell carries out normal functions, but also prepares to divide. The cell's **DNA** is unravelled and **replicated**, to double its genetic content. The **organelles** are also **replicated** so it has spare ones, and its ATP content is increased (ATP provides the energy needed for cell division).

Interphase

Cell
Chromosome
Cytoplasm
Nucleus
Centriole

Unravelled DNA containing two copies of each chromosome

1) **Prophase** — The **chromosomes condense**, getting shorter and fatter. Tiny bundles of protein called **centrioles** start moving to opposite ends of the cell, forming a network of protein fibres across it called the **spindle**. The **nuclear envelope** (the membrane around the nucleus) **breaks down** and chromosomes lie free in the cytoplasm.

Centrioles move to opposite ends of the cell

Nuclear envelope starts to break down

Centromere

As mitosis begins, the chromosomes are made of two strands joined in the middle by a <u>centromere</u>. The separate strands are called <u>chromatids</u>.

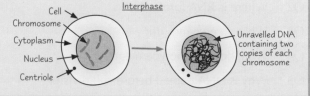

One chromatid — Centromere
Sister chromatids

There are two strands because each chromosome has already made an <u>identical copy</u> of itself during <u>interphase</u>. When mitosis is over, the chromatids end up as one-strand chromosomes in the new daughter cells.

The Cell Cycle and Mitosis

2) <u>Metaphase</u> — The chromosomes (each with two chromatids) **line up** along the middle of the cell and become **attached** to the **spindle** by their **centromere**.

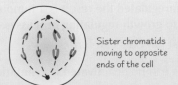

Spindle fibres

Centromeres on spindle equator

So long and thanks for all the organelles!

It's so hard letting go of my baby girls. It feels like a part of me has gone with them.

There, there love — it's all part of the cycle of life.

Mitosis can be a moving time.

3) <u>Anaphase</u> — The centromeres divide, **separating** each pair of sister **chromatids**. The spindles contract, pulling chromatids to opposite ends of the cell, centromere first.

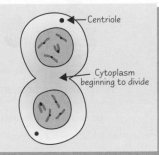

Sister chromatids moving to opposite ends of the cell

4) <u>Telophase</u> — The chromatids reach the **opposite poles** on the spindle. They uncoil and become long and thin again. They're now called **chromosomes** again. A **nuclear envelope** forms around each group of chromosomes, so there are now **two nuclei**. The **cytoplasm divides** and there are now **two daughter cells** that are **genetically identical** to the original cell and to each other. Mitosis is finished and each daughter cell starts the **interphase** part of the cell cycle to get ready for the next round of mitosis.

Centriole

Cytoplasm beginning to divide

You can **Observe Mitosis** by **Staining Chromosomes**

You can **stain chromosomes** so you can see them under a **microscope**. This means you can watch what happens to them **during mitosis** — and it makes high-adrenaline viewing, I can tell you. You need to be able to **recognise** each stage in mitosis from diagrams and **photographs** — lucky you. You've seen the diagrams, now enjoy the photos:

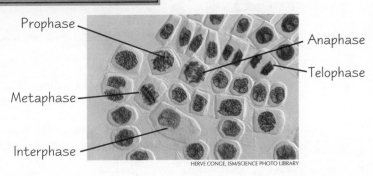

Prophase

Anaphase

Telophase

Metaphase

Interphase

HERVE CONGE, ISM/SCIENCE PHOTO LIBRARY

Practice Questions

Q1 List the four main stages of the cell cycle.

Q2 Give the two main uses of mitosis.

Q3 List in order the four stages of mitosis.

Exam Question

Q1 The diagrams show cells at different stages of mitosis.

Cell A

Cell B

Cell C

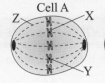

Z — X
Y

a) For each of the cells A, B and C state the stage of mitosis, giving a reason for your answer. [6 marks]

b) Name the structures labelled X, Y and Z in cell A. [3 marks]

<u>Doctor, Doctor, I'm getting short and fat — don't worry, it's just a phase...</u>

Quite a lot to learn in this topic — but it's all dead important stuff, so no slacking. Most body cells undergo mitosis — it's how they multiply and how organisms like us grow and develop. Remember that chromosomes during mitosis are made up of two sister chromatids joined by a centromere. Nice to know family values are important to genetic material too.

Cancer

Cancer is a disease that affects people of all ages, animals and even plants. There are lots of different types of cancer, but they all involve uncontrolled cell growth and all have potentially devastating effects.

Mutations in Genes Can Cause Uncontrolled Cell Growth

1) Cell growth and cell division are **controlled by genes**.

2) These genes contain instructions for making **proteins** that **regulate** cell growth and division.

3) If a cell grows and divides **unregulated** the result is a **tumour** — a mass of abnormal cells. Tumour cells **don't** respond to **growth regulating processes**.

4) There are **two** main ways that tumours can form:

1) **Tumour suppressor genes** can be **deactivated** if a **mutation** occurs in the DNA sequence.

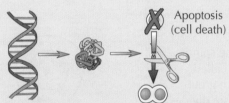

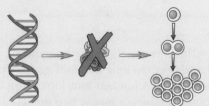

When functioning normally, tumour suppressor genes produce proteins that **stop cells dividing** or cause them to **self-destruct** (apoptosis).

If a **mutation** occurs in a tumour suppressor gene, the protein **isn't produced** and cells grow **uncontrollably**, resulting in a tumour.

2) There's a **mutation** in the DNA of **growth promotion genes**.

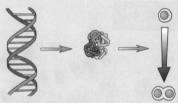

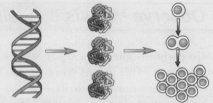

When functioning normally, growth promotion genes produce proteins that **make cells divide**.

If a **mutation** occurs in the growth promotion gene it can become **extra active**. This causes cells to divide **uncontrollably**, resulting in a tumour.

5) Tumours are caused by **multiple mutations** in **lots** of different genes.

A Carcinogen is Any Substance That Causes Cells to Become Cancerous

Some substances can cause **mutations in DNA**. Anything that causes a mutation that could lead to **cancer** is called a **carcinogen**. There are a number of things that can cause **mutations** in growth controlling genes:

1) **Chemicals** — e.g. the chemicals in cigarette smoke.
2) **Radiation** — e.g. ultraviolet radiation from the Sun.

Some mutations also occur spontaneously, due to errors in DNA replication.

Tumour Cells Look and Function Differently to Normal Cells

Tumour cells **can differ** from normal cells in many **different ways**:

1) They have an **irregular shape**.

2) The **nucleus** is **larger** and **darker** than in normal cells. Sometimes the cells have more than one nucleus.

3) They don't produce all the proteins needed to function correctly.

4) They have **different antigens** on their **surface** (see p. 36).

5) They don't respond to **growth regulating processes**.

6) They divide (by mitosis) **more frequently** than normal cells.

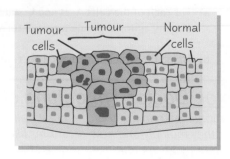

Tumour cells   Tumour   Normal cells

Cancer

Tumours can be Benign or Malignant (Cancerous)

Tumours can develop for **years** without any obvious symptoms and can be quite **large** by the time they're discovered.
Not all tumours are **cancerous** — there are **two** different types:

1) **Malignant tumours** are **cancers**. They usually grow **rapidly** and **invade** and **destroy** surrounding tissues. Cells can break off the tumours and **spread** to other parts of the body (see below).

2) **Benign tumours** are not cancerous. They usually grow **slower** than malignant tumours and are often covered in **fibrous tissue** that stops cells invading other tissues. Benign tumours are often **harmless**, but they can cause **blockages** and put **pressure** on organs. Some benign tumours can become **malignant**.

Cancer Cells Spread by Metastasis

Cancer cells in malignant tumours can **spread** to other parts of the body by a process called **metastasis**.

1) Cells break off the **primary (original) tumour** (e.g. in the breast).

2) Cells enter the **bloodstream** (or **lymphatic system**).

3) Cancer cells continue to **divide** in the bloodstream (or lymphatic system).

4) Cells **invade** other tissues or organs (e.g. the lungs).

5) Cells form **secondary (new) tumours**.

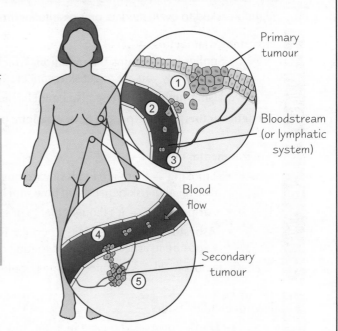

Practice Questions

Q1   Name two things that can cause mutations in DNA.

Q2   What name is given to the spread of cancer cells from one organ to another?

Q3   Name two ways that cancer cells can be transported from one organ to another.

Exam Questions

Q1   Mandy has been diagnosed with cancer. The doctor tells her she has a malignant tumour in her left breast and a secondary malignant tumour in her left ulna (one of the bones in her arm).

    a) Describe two differences between benign and malignant tumours.   [2 marks]

    b) Describe how cancer cells can spread from the breast to the ulna.   [5 marks]

    c) Describe how tumours can arise from mutations in DNA.   [5 marks]

Q2   Give four ways in which tumour cells can look or function differently from normal cells.   [4 marks]

Remember, only malignant tumours are cancerous...

You need to understand the difference between benign and malignant. You should never, ever say benign cancers — there's no such thing as a benign cancer. Only malignant tumours are cancerous. And don't forget about metastasis — the process by which a primary (original) tumour spreads to produce a secondary (new) tumour.

Interpreting Cancer Data

Now you know what cancer is, it's time to take a closer look at what increases your risk of getting it.

Genetic and Environmental Factors Affect the Risk of Cancer

There's **no single cause** for cancer but scientists have identified lots of different '**risk factors**' — things that **increase** a person's **chance** of getting cancer. Risk factors can be either **genetic** or **environmental**:

1) **Genetic factors** — some cancers are linked with **specific inherited alleles**. If you **inherit** that allele you're **more likely** to get that type of cancer (but it **doesn't mean** you'll **definitely** get that type of cancer).

2) **Environmental factors** — exposure to **radiation**, **lifestyle choices** such as **smoking**, increased **alcohol consumption**, and a **high-fat diet** have all been **linked** to an increased chance of developing some cancers.

You might be asked to evaluate data on possible **factors** associated with skin, lung or bowel cancer:

Skin cancer

Environmental factors —
- **Sunlight** — contains **UV radiation**, which **causes mutations**. The more time you spend in the Sun the more likely you are to get skin cancer. The risk can be **reduced**, e.g. by using **sunblock** and **covering up**.
- Using **sunbeds** — these also emit UV radiation.

Genetic factors — some people have a **genetic predisposition** to the disease.

> Age is a risk factor for most cancers — the older you are the more likely your DNA has developed a mutation in a gene that could lead to cancer.

Lung cancer

Environmental factors —
- **Smoking** — there are loads of **carcinogens** (see p. 52) in **cigarette smoke**. The level of risk depends on **how much** you smoke and **how long** you've smoked for.
- **Air pollution** — it's thought that exposure to exhaust fumes increases the risk of lung cancer.
- **Asbestos** — this used to be a popular **building material**. However it was discovered that exposure to asbestos can lead to lung cancer.

Genetic factors — like skin cancer, some people also have a **genetic predisposition** to the disease.

Colon cancer

Environmental factors —
- **Diet** — people who eat a **high-fat**, **low-fibre** diet have an increased risk.
- **Smoking** — people who smoke are more likely to suffer from the disease.

Genetic factors — again, like skin and lung cancer, colon cancer has a **genetic component**.

There are Ethical Issues Associated with Treating Smoking-Related Diseases

About 90% of lung cancers are **tobacco-related** and many other **diseases** are linked to smoking. This has led to some heated debates about the **treatment of smoking-related** diseases.

1) Smokers' health problems are **self-inflicted**, so some people think the NHS **shouldn't** treat them. This would **save** a lot of **money**. But everyone **pays** for the NHS through taxes, including smokers. Smokers may even **pay more** than most due to additional **taxes on cigarettes**.

2) A similar argument could be made for people who do risky sports like **base jumping**. Any injuries they get are **self-inflicted** — they take a risk (like smokers do) and if they get injured we still treat them.

3) Also, it's impossible to tell if a disease is **definitely** caused by smoking — there could be other **genetic** or **environmental** factors involved. Some people think that it'd be unfair not to treat them because it might not have been caused by smoking.

Some people think **smoking tobacco** should be **made illegal**.

1) Making smoking **illegal** would **reduce** the incidence of smoking-related diseases and **save lives**.

2) Some people think we should be allowed to **decide for ourselves**.

3) Some people think that we shouldn't ban smoking because we don't ban **alcohol** or **DIY** (which count for a **high percentage** of the injuries treated in hospitals every day).

Manuel doesn't care that 200 000 people are treated for DIY injuries each year. He just loves to hammer.

Interpreting Cancer Data

You need to be Able to *Interpret Data* on *Cancer* and *Risk Factors*

Here are the results of a couple of studies to take a look at:

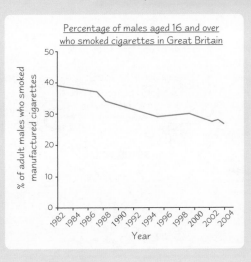

Percentage of males aged 16 and over who smoked cigarettes in Great Britain

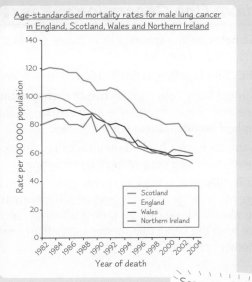

Age-standardised mortality rates for male lung cancer in England, Scotland, Wales and Northern Ireland

See pages 82-84 for more on interpreting data.

You might be asked to:

1) **Explain the data** — The graph on the left shows that the **number** of adult males in Great Britain (England, Wales and Scotland) who **smoke decreased** between 1982 and 2004. The graph on the right shows that the male lung cancer **mortality rate decreased** between 1982 and 2004 for each of the countries shown.

2) **Draw conclusions** — You need to be careful what you say here. There's a **correlation** (link) between the **number** of males **who smoked** and the **mortality rate** for male lung cancer. But you **can't** say that one **caused** the other. There could be **other reasons** for the trend, e.g. deaths due to lung cancer may have decreased because less asbestos was being used in homes (not because fewer people were smoking).

3) **Evaluate the methodology** — The graph on the right shows mortality (**death**) rates. The rate of **cases** of lung cancer **may have been increasing** but medical advances may mean more people were **surviving** (so only mortality was decreasing). Some information about the **people involved** in the studies would be helpful. For example, did both studies use similar groups? E.g. similar diet, occupation, alcohol consumption etc. If they didn't then the results might not be reliable.

Practice Questions

Q1 What two broad categories do most risk factors for cancer fall into?

Q2 Describe the ethical issues surrounding the treatment of smoking-related diseases.

Exam Question

Q1 The table below shows data from a study of 175 000 people into risk factors for malignant melanoma (skin cancer).

a) What conclusion can be drawn from the data? [1 mark]

b) Explain why it is important to observe such a large sample of people. [1 mark]

c) Suggest a reason for the result. [2 marks]

No. of cases of severe sunburn	Relative risk of malignant melanoma
0	1
1-2	1.4
3-5	1.62
6-9	1.95
10+	2.36

Don't let your personal opinion sway your ethical arguments...

You could easily get a question about the ethics surrounding the treatment of smokers and smoking-related diseases. Don't let your personal opinion about smoking affect your argument. You need to show that you understand all sides of the problem and the pros and cons of any ideas that may be put forward.

Meiosis

More cell division — lovely jubbly. Meiosis is the type of cell division that produces gametes — the sex cells that come together at fertilisation to form a new organism.

DNA from One Generation is Passed to the Next by Gametes

1) **Gametes** are the **sperm** cells in males and **ova** (egg cells) in females.

2) They **join together** at **fertilisation** to form a **zygote**.

3) Normal **body cells** contain **two** of **each chromosome**, one from the mum and one from the dad — this is the **diploid number** (**2n**) of chromosomes.

4) **Gametes** have a **haploid** (**n**) number of chromosomes — there's only **one** copy of each chromosome.

5) At **fertilisation**, a **haploid sperm** (n) fuses with a **haploid egg** (n), making a cell (zygote) with the **normal diploid number** of chromosomes (2n). Half these chromosomes are from the father (the sperm) and half are from the mother (the egg).

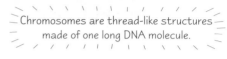

Chromosomes are thread-like structures made of one long DNA molecule.

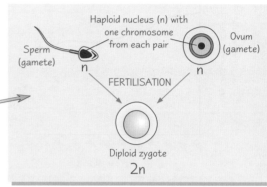

Meiosis Halves the Chromosome Number

1) **Meiosis** is a type of **cell division**.

2) Cells in the testes (in men) and ovaries (in women) divide by meiosis to **produce gametes**. The cells are **diploid** to start with, but the cells that are formed are **haploid** — the chromosome number **halves**.

3) This makes sure cells have a **constant number** of chromosomes through the **generations** — without meiosis, you'd get **double** the number of chromosomes when the gametes fused. Not good.

There are Two Divisions in Meiosis

The starting cell contains both chromosomes from each **homologous pair** (see page 47) — that's 23 homologous pairs, **46** chromosomes in total (two 1's, two 2's, two 3's etc.). Each of the four cells produced (**daughter cells**) has only **one chromosome** from each homologous pair — that's 23 chromosomes in total (one 1, one 2, one 3, etc.).

1) The DNA unravels and **replicates** so there are **two** copies of **each** chromosome, called **chromatids**. So, you've got **2 × 2n** chromosomes.

2) The DNA condenses to form double-armed chromosomes, made from **two sister chromatids**.

3) The chromosomes arrange themselves into **homologous pairs**.

4) **Meiosis I** (first division) — the homologous pairs of each chromosome are separated, **halving** the chromosome number. Now you've got **2n** chromosomes in each cell.

5) **Meiosis II** (second division) — the pairs of sister **chromatids** that make up each chromosome are separated — halving the chromosome number again. This gives **n** chromosomes in each cell.

6) **Four haploid cells** (gametes) that are **genetically different** from each other are produced.

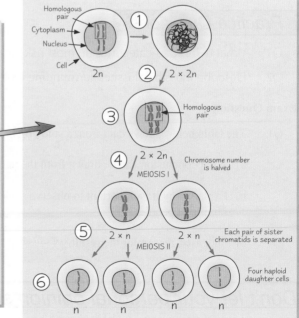

We've only shown 4 chromosomes here for simplicity. Humans actually have 46 (23 homologous pairs).

Meiosis

Chromosome Mutations are Caused by Errors in Cell Division

1) When meiosis **works properly**, all four daughter cells will end up with **23 whole chromosomes**, one from each homologous pair (1 to 23).

2) But sometimes meiosis **goes wrong** and the cells produced contain **variations** in the numbers of whole chromosomes or **parts** of chromosomes.

3) For example, two cells might have 23 whole chromosomes, one each of 1 to 23, but the other two might get a bit muddled up, one having two chromosome 6's and the other no chromosome 6.

4) This is called **chromosome mutation** and is caused by **errors** during meiosis.

5) Chromosome mutations lead to **inherited conditions** because the errors are present in the **gametes** (the hereditary cells).

One type of chromosome mutation, **non-disjunction**, leads to **Down syndrome**:

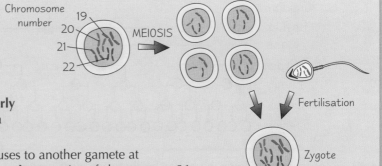

1) About **95%** of **Down syndrome** cases are caused by a person having an **extra copy** of **chromosome 21**.

2) It's caused by **non-disjunction** of the chromosomes.

3) Chromosome 21 **fails** to **separate properly** during meiosis, so one cell gets an extra copy of 21 and another gets none.

4) When the gamete with the **extra copy** fuses to another gamete at **fertilisation** the resulting zygote will have **three** copies of chromosome 21.

Practice Questions

Q1 Explain what is meant by the terms haploid and diploid.

Q2 What happens to the chromosome number at fertilisation?

Q3 How many divisions are there in meiosis?

Q4 How many daughter cells are produced from one parent cell by meiosis?

Q5 What is a chromosome mutation?

Exam Questions

Q1 Explain why it's important for gametes to have half the number of chromosomes as normal body cells. [2 marks]

Q2 The diagram opposite shows human cell fertilisation. How many chromosomes would be found in cells A, B and C? [3 marks]

Q3 a) Describe how chromosome mutation leads to Down syndrome. [3 marks]

b) What name is given to the type of chromosome mutation that causes Down syndrome? [1 mark]

Reproduction isn't as exciting as some people would have you believe...

*This stuff can take a while to sink in — but that's no excuse to sit there staring at the page muttering things like "I don't get it" and "guinea pigs don't have to learn this stuff — I wish I was a guinea pig". Use the diagrams to help you understand — they look evil, but they really help. The key thing is to understand what happens to the **number of chromosomes** in meiosis.*

Classification

For hundreds of years people have been putting organisms into groups to make it easier to recognise and name them. It's not just done for animals and plants though — us (humans) and our distant relatives (past human species that are now dead) have been classified too.

Classification is All About Grouping Together Similar Organisms

Classification involves **naming** organisms and **organising them** into **groups** based on their **similarities**. This makes it **easier** for scientists to **identify** them and to **study** them.

1) There are seven levels of groups used in classification (called taxonomic groups).

2) **Similar organisms** are first sorted into **large groups** called **kingdoms**, e.g. all animals are in the animal kingdom.

3) **Similar** organisms from that kingdom are then grouped into a **phylum**. **Similar** organisms from each phylum are then grouped into a **class**, and **so on** down the seven levels of the hierarchy.

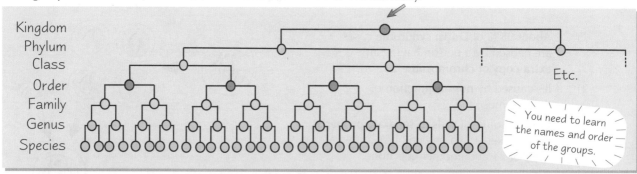

Kingdom
Phylum
Class
Order
Family
Genus
Species

Etc.

You need to learn the names and order of the groups.

4) As you move **down** the hierarchy, there are **more groups** at each level but **fewer organisms** in each group,

5) The hierarchy **ends** with **species** — the groups that contain only **one type** of organism (e.g. humans, dogs, *E. coli*). You need to **learn** the definition of a **species**:

> **A species is a group of similar organisms able to reproduce to give fertile offspring.**

Species are given a **scientific name** to **distinguish** them from similar organisms. This is a **two-word** name in **Latin**. The **first** word is the **genus** name and the **second** word is the **species** name — e.g. humans are *Homo sapiens*. Giving organisms a scientific name enables scientists to **communicate** about organisms in a standard way that minimises confusion. E.g. Americans call a type of bird **cockatoos** and Australians call them **flaming galahs** (best said with an Australian accent), but it's the **same bird**. If the correct **scientific name** is used — *Eolophus roseicapillus* — there's no confusion.

Humans are Classified as Homo Sapiens

This column shows the features that have been used to classify humans into each of these groups.

Here's how **humans** are classified:

		FEATURES
KINGDOM	**Animalia**	Animal
PHYLUM	**Chordata**	Has a nerve cord
CLASS	**Mammalia**	Feeds young on milk, has hair / fur, sweat glands
ORDER	**Primates**	Five digits with opposable thumb, modified claws, reduced snout, binocular vision
FAMILY	**Hominidae**	Short face, capability for language (including limited and unspoken forms), no prehensile tail
GENUS	*Homo*	Very similar DNA to modern humans, narrow nasal septum, pelvis adapted for bipedalism
SPECIES	*sapiens*	Cranial capacity around 1350 cm^3, spoken language.

Classification

Classification is NOT Just Based on Observable Features...

1) Early classification systems **only** used **observable features** (things you can see) to place organisms into groups, e.g. number of legs, whether they lay eggs, whether they can do the hokey-cokey...

2) But this method has **problems**. Scientists don't always agree on the **relative importance** of different features and groups based **solely** on **physical features** may not show how **related** organisms are. ⟶

> For example, **sharks** and **whales look** quite similar and they both **live** in the sea. But they're **not** actually closely related.

3) Classification systems are **now** based on observable features **along** with **other evidence** (see below).

4) This means organisms are now grouped according to **phylogenetic relationships** (how related they are to each other) — species are put into groups with other species that they're **related to**. This allows you to look at the groups and see how **closely** related different organisms are.

...Evidence from a Range of Sources is Used

The **more similar** organisms are, the **more related** they are. We now use a range of evidence to see how **similar**, and therefore how related, organisms are. The type of evidence used to **classify organisms** now includes:

1) **Biochemical evidence** — the similarities in **proteins** and **DNA**. **More closely related** organisms will have **more similar** molecules. E.g. skunks were in the family Mustelidae until biochemical studies showed their DNA was very different to other members of that family but was similar to members of the family Mephitidae, so they were reclassified.

2) **Embryological evidence** — the similarities in the **early stages** of an organism's **development**. E.g. fish and salamander embryos are more similar and so more closely related than salamander and turtle embryos. ⟶

Fish Salamander Turtle

3) **Anatomical evidence** — the similarities in **structure** and **function** of different body parts. E.g. similarities in the **skeletal structure** of different mammals supports the classification of these animals into the same class.

The forelimbs of three mammals:

Orangutan Dog Tapir

4) **Behavioural evidence** — e.g. the brown lemur (*Eulemur fulvus*) and the black lemur (*Eulemur macaco*) are anatomically and genetically very similar, but show a lot of difference in their **social organisation**.

5) **Immunological evidence** — the similarities in the **immune system**. E.g. **antibodies** and **antigens** in human blood are similar to those in chimpanzee blood. Humans and chimpanzees are members of the same family.

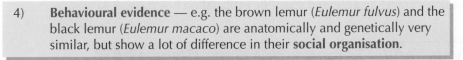

Practice Questions

Q1 What is the definition of a species?

Q2 List the seven taxonomic groups in order.

Exam Questions

Q1 Complete the table to show the classification of humans.

	Phylum			Family		Species
Animalia		Mammalia	Primates		Homo	

[7 marks]

Q2 Give two forms of evidence that can be used in the classification of organisms. [2 marks]

<u>Using behavioural evidence, my brother is a totally different species...</u>

It's a pretty good idea to make sure that you really understand all the basics on these pages before delving any deeper into this section. If you don't understand what a species is, you'll find yourself struggling later on. I know you know it really... a species is a group of similar organisms able to reproduce to give fertile offspring... Now, don't forget that.

Evolution

Evolution is the slow and continual change of organisms from one generation to the next. Darwin came up with a theory to explain how this change comes about and although it's really old, it's still going strong...

Darwin Published his Theory of Evolution by Natural Selection in 1859

Scientists use **theories** to attempt to **explain** their **observations** — Charles Darwin was no exception. Darwin wrote his theory of evolution by natural selection to explain some of his observations about the world around him.

Observations:

1) Organisms produce **more offspring** than **survive**.
2) There's **variation** between members of the **same species**.
3) **Characteristics** can be **passed on** from one generation to the next.

Natural selection is one process by which evolution occurs.

Theory:

1) Individuals within a population **show variation** in their **phenotypes** (their characteristics).
2) **Predation**, **disease** and **competition** create a **struggle for survival**.
3) Individuals with **better adaptations** (characteristics that give a selective advantage, e.g. being able to run away from predators faster) are **more likely** to **survive**, **reproduce** and **pass on** their advantageous adaptations to their **offspring**.
4) Over time, the **number** of individuals with the advantageous adaptations **increases**.
5) Over generations this leads to **evolution** as the favourable adaptations become **more common** in the population.

It was later realised that some **variation in phenotype** is due to **genetic variation**. Different individuals have **different alleles** (different **versions** of **genes**, see p. 47). Individuals with **advantageous characteristics** are more likely to survive, reproduce and pass on their advantageous alleles to the **next generation**.

Sid and Nancy were well adapted to hiding in candy-floss shops.

At first, there was some **opposition** to Darwin's theory as it conflicted with some **religious beliefs**. Over time the theory has become **increasingly accepted** as more **evidence** has been found to support it and no evidence has been shown to disprove it. Evidence increases scientists' **confidence** in a theory — the more evidence there is, the more chance of something becoming an **accepted scientific explanation** (see pages 2-3).

An Earlier Theory of Evolution by Lamarck Has Been Disproved

In the early 1800s, Jean-Baptiste Lamarck developed a different evolutionary theory to explain his observations.
Observations:

1) Many organisms are well **adapted** to their environment.
2) Individuals can **develop** useful characteristics — e.g. build greater muscle strength.
3) Characteristics can be **passed on** from one generation to the next.

Theory:

1) Individual organisms **change** over **their lifetime** to become **better adapted** to their environment — they **lose** characteristics they don't use, and **develop** characteristics that are useful.
2) Organisms pass these changes on to their **offspring**.
3) Over generations this process causes **evolution**.

A scientist provided scientific evidence that helped to disprove the idea that acquired traits could be inherited. He carried out an experiment in which he chopped off the tails of 1500 mice over 20 generations. He discovered that no offspring were ever born without a tail.

Lamarckian evolution was once widely accepted — but when Darwin's theory was published many scientists felt it provided a **better explanation** of the observations. Later, advances in genetics clarified the difference between **inherited** and **environmental** characteristics, and disproved the idea that **traits acquired** during your lifetime, e.g. a pierced ear, could be inherited by your children. This sort of thing happens all the time in science — scientific knowledge **changes** when **new evidence** or a **new theory** that provides a better explanation comes along (see pages 2-3).

Evolution

Evolution by Natural Selection Leads to Change Within a Population

In the exam you might have to explain how natural selection can produce changes in a population.
Here are a couple of examples to show you how natural selection leads to change:

Example 1

Scientists have observed the evolution of **antibiotic resistance** in many species of **bacteria**. For example, four years after the antibiotic penicillin became widely available, strains of *Staphylococcus aureus* were shown to be **resistant** to it. A **new antibiotic** (methicillin) was introduced, but resistance to this drug began appearing too (MRSA — methicillin-resistant *Staphylococcus aureus*). Since then a series of new antibiotics have been introduced (tetracycline, erythromycin, vancomycin, etc.), but each time populations of bacteria have **evolved resistance**.

The **evolution** of antibiotic resistance can be explained by **natural selection**:

1) There is **variation** in a population of bacteria. **Genetic mutations** make some bacteria naturally **resistant** to an antibiotic than others.

2) If the population of bacteria is exposed to that antibiotic, only the individuals with resistance will **survive** to **reproduce**.

3) The **alleles** that cause the antibiotic resistance will be **passed on** to the next generation, and so the population will evolve to become resistant to the drug.

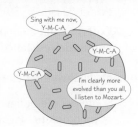

Example 2

In 1810 a herd of **caribou** were taken from the Arctic to an area with a **warmer climate**. In 1810 the average **fur length** of the caribou was 3.5 cm. In **1960** the average fur length was found to be 2.1 cm.

The change in **fur length** can be explained by **natural selection**:

1) There is **variation** in **fur length** in the population of caribou.

2) Caribou with **shorter fur** will be **better adapted** to the warmer climate as they'll be less likely to overheat. These caribou will be **more likely to survive** and **reproduce**.

3) The **alleles** for shorter fur length will be more likely to be **passed on** to the next generation, and so the population will gradually get shorter and shorter fur.

Practice Questions

Q1 Suggest one observation that led Darwin to suggest his theory of evolution.

Q2 Describe Darwin's theory of evolution by natural selection.

Q3 Suggest one observation that led Lamarck to suggest his theory of evolution.

Q4 Describe Lamarck's theory of evolution.

Exam Question

Q1 The bat *Anoura fistulata* has a very long tongue (up to one and a half times the length of its body). The tongue enables the bat to feed on the nectar inside a deep tubular flower found in the forests of Ecuador.

    a) i) Describe how Lamarck's theory of evolution would explain the evolution of such a long tongue.   [2 marks]

       ii) Explain what part of Lamarck's theory has been proved wrong.   [1 mark]

    b) Describe how Darwin's theory of evolution by natural selection can explain the evolution of such a long tongue.   [3 marks]

Oh, generations, I see — I was hoping to develop superpowers overnight...

It's important to realise that no scientific knowledge is set in stone. If some new evidence comes along, or another scientist comes up with a better explanation for something, things will change. The theories for evolution are a good example of this — Lamarck's theory had plenty of followers until Darwin's theory came along and provided a better explanation.

Evidence for Evolution

There's plenty of evidence out there for evolution — including the fossil record and experimental evidence.

Not everyone Agrees with Darwin's Theory of Evolution

The **theory** of evolution explains how all organisms came about and it's backed up by tons of **evidence**. Some people don't agree with the theory of evolution though. They believe that the origin and diversity of organisms can be explained in **other ways**. But so far there's **no evidence** to support these other ways or evidence to **disprove** evolution.

Evidence for the theory of evolution includes:

1) **The fossil record** — fossils are the **remains** of organisms **preserved in rocks**. By arranging fossils in chronological (date) order, **gradual changes** in organisms can be observed that provide **evidence** of evolution.

2) Information on how **related** organisms are from **anatomical**, **physiological**, **embryological** and **biochemical** evidence (see p. 59).

3) **Experimental evidence** — evolution has been **observed** in some organisms, e.g. the development of **antibiotic resistance** in bacteria (see p. 61).

Arguments against the theory of evolution include:

1) Some people believe the evidence for the theory of evolution is **unreliable**, **inconsistent** or **incomplete**. E.g. the fossil record contains **missing links** between related species. But this is only an **absence** of evidence, it doesn't disprove the theory of evolution.

2) Some people also argue that the theory of evolution doesn't explain the development of some **complex structures** and **behaviours**. However, evolutionary theories that **can** explain these characteristics have been put forward by other people.

You Need to be Able to Objectively Evaluate Evidence for Evolution

Here are two examples of some evidence that supports the theory of evolution:

The Fossil Record — The Horse

Suggested evolution of the horse

1) A good fossil record of the **horse** is found in **North America**.

2) Between the earliest fossil remains of *Hyracotherium* (an early horse-like mammal) in rock dating from 60 million years ago, and *Equus* (the modern horse), there are many **different species** that show a **gradual change** of characteristics:

- Increasing **size**
- Lengthening of **limbs and feet**
- **Hoof** development
- Increasing **tooth** size

3) These changes can be explained as **adaptations** to a **changing environment** from marshy woodland to open grassland. E.g. **hoofed feet** would enable horses to run away from predators **more quickly** and so they'd be more likely to **survive**, **reproduce** and pass on their **genes**.

4) One **limitation** of fossil record evidence is that it can have **gaps** — places where a **large evolutionary change** suggests 'in-between' species for which we've not yet found fossils. Another problem is that records can stretch over **millions of years** and sometimes over **multiple continents**, making them difficult to piece together.

Experimental Evidence — Peppered Moths

A study of **peppered moths** in England between 1850 and 1900 showed that the colour of the majority of moths changed from light to dark. During this time, **pollution** had **blackened** the trees that the moths lived on. Scientists explained the change by suggesting that the dark coloured moths would have been better **camouflaged** from predators, so would be more likely to **survive**, reproduce and pass on the alleles for dark colouring.

That colour is marvellous on you, really darling.

Evidence for Evolution

Fossil Evidence can be Dated in Two Ways

① Stratigraphy

1) Stratigraphy is the study of **rock layers**.
2) It can tell you the **relative ages** of fossils in rocks — which fossils are **older** and which are **younger**.
3) Older rocks are generally found **below** younger rocks. →

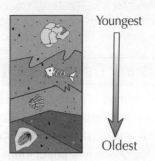

Youngest

Oldest

② Radiometric Dating

Radiometric dating uses naturally occurring **radioactive isotopes** with known **decay rates**. These isotopes decay from a parent isotope to a daughter isotope at a certain rate. By comparing the **relative abundance** of the parent and daughter isotopes in a rock or fossil its age can be determined.

There are **two types** of radiometric dating you need to know about:

1) **Carbon Dating** involves measuring the **ratio** of **carbon-14** and **carbon-12** in rocks and fossils that contain carbon. Carbon has a **fast** rate of decay, making it suitable for dating rocks and fossils **less than 60 000 years old**.

2) **Potassium-Argon Dating** involves measuring the **ratio** of **potassium-40** and **argon-40** in rocks. Potassium-40 is found in many sedimentary rocks, and slowly decays to argon 40 — so over time the relative amount of argon-40 will increase. Potassium has a **slow** rate of decay, making it suitable for dating rocks **over 100 000 years old**.

Marie's outfit was dated 1986.

Practice Questions

Q1 Name two forms of evidence that support the theory of evolution.

Q2 Explain how the relative age of fossils can be determined using stratigraphy.

Q3 Name two types of radiometric dating used for dating fossils.

Exam Question

Q1 The fossil record showing the evolution of the hand of the now extinct lesser spotted snozcumber is shown on the right. Two million years ago the snozcumber ancestor walked on four legs and grazed on open grassland. The most recent snozcumber species lived in forests and had a mixed diet of fruit and vegetables.

2.5 million years ago   2 million years ago   100 000 years ago

a) Describe the evolutionary change shown in the fossil record and suggest an explanation for it. [2 marks]

b) Suggest any problems associated with this fossil record. [2 marks]

Potassium-Argon dating — they make a great couple...

If you're asked to evaluate a piece of evidence for evolution, it's really important that you think about how it supports the theory and look for any gaps in the evidence. But remember a gap in the fossil record doesn't disprove the theory of evolution — it just shows up a place where evidence has yet to be found.

Speciation

The formation of new species has resulted in all the diversity we see around us. For example, it's thought there could be 30 million different species of insect in the world, including the Aha ha *(an Australian wasp) and the* Colon rectum *(a type of beetle)... and no, I didn't make those up if you were wondering.*

Speciation *is the Development of a* New Species

1) A **species** is defined as a group of similar organisms that can **reproduce** and produce **fertile offspring**.

2) Species can exist as **one** or **more populations**, e.g. there are populations of the American black bear (*Ursus americanus*) in parts of America and in parts of Canada.

3) Speciation happens when **populations** of the **same species** become **reproductively isolated**.

Geographical Isolation *and* Natural Selection *Lead to* Speciation

1) Geographical isolation happens when a **physical barrier divides** a population of a species — **floods**, **volcanic eruptions** and **earthquakes** can all cause barriers that isolate some individuals from the main population.

2) **Conditions** on either side of the barrier will be slightly **different**. For example, there might be a **different climate** on each side.

3) Because the environment is **different** on each side, different **characteristics** (phenotypes) will become more common due to natural selection:

- Because different **adaptations** will be **advantageous** on each side, the **allele frequencies** will change in each population, e.g. if one allele is more advantageous on one side of the barrier, the frequency of that allele on that side will **increase**.
- **Mutations** will take place **independently** in each population, also changing the **allele frequencies**.
- The changes in allele frequencies will lead to changes in **phenotype frequencies**, e.g. the advantageous adaptations (**phenotypes**) will become more common on that side.

4) Eventually, individuals from different populations will have changed so much that they won't be able to breed with one another to produce **fertile** offspring — they'll have become **reproductively isolated**.

5) The two groups will have become separate **species**.

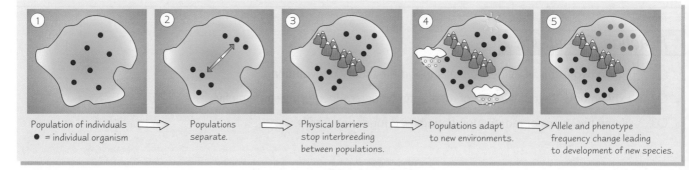

Population of individuals
● = individual organism

⟹ Populations separate.

⟹ Physical barriers stop interbreeding between populations.

⟹ Populations adapt to new environments.

⟹ Allele and phenotype frequency change leading to development of new species.

Reproductive Isolation *Occurs in Many Ways*

Reproductive isolation occurs because the **changes** in the alleles and phenotypes of the two populations **prevent** them from **successfully breeding together**. These changes include:

1) **Seasonal changes** — individuals from the same population develop different **flowering** or **mating** seasons, or become **sexually active** at different times of the year.

2) **Mechanical changes** — changes in **genitalia** prevent successful mating.

3) **Behavioural changes** — a group of individuals develop **courtship rituals** that **aren't attractive** to the main population.

Janice's courtship ritual was still successful in attracting mates.

A population **doesn't** have to become **geographically isolated** to become **reproductively isolated**. Random mutations could occur **within a population**, resulting in the changes mentioned above, **preventing** members of that population breeding with each other.

Speciation

Speciation has Resulted in a Great Diversity of Organisms

1) The diversity of life on Earth today is the result of **millions of speciation events**.

2) To start with there was **one population** of organisms. The population was **divided** and the new populations evolved into **separate species**.

3) The new species were then **divided again** and the new populations evolved into more separate species.

4) This process has been **repeated** over a long period of time to create millions of new species.

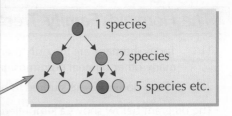

Here's an example to show you how multiple speciation events resulted in the formation of 14 species of finch from one common ancestor:

Darwin's finches

Darwin observed 14 species of finch on the **Galapagos Islands** — a group of islands found near the equator in the Pacific Ocean. Each species of finch was unique to a single island. Although the finches were similar, the size and shape of their **beaks** differed — they were adapted to the **food sources** found on their specific island. Darwin theorised that:

1) All the species of finch had a **common ancestor**.

2) Different populations became **isolated** on different islands.

3) Each population **evolved adaptations** to their environment.

4) The populations eventually evolved into **separate species**.

Practice Questions

Q1 How can geographical isolation result in speciation?

Q2 What is reproductive isolation?

Exam Question

Q1 The diagram shows an experiment conducted with fruit flies. One population was split in two and each population was fed a different food. After many generations the two populations were placed together and it was observed that they were unable to breed together.

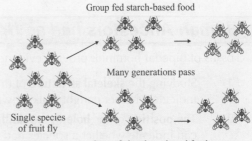

a) What evidence shows that speciation occurred? [1 mark]

b) Explain why the experiment resulted in speciation. [3 marks]

c) Suggest two possible reasons why members of the two populations were not able to breed together. [2 marks]

d) During the experiment, populations of fruit flies were artificially isolated. Suggest one way that populations of organisms could become isolated naturally. [1 mark]

e) Describe the effect of speciation on the diversity of life. [1 mark]

Chess club members — self-enforced reproductive isolation...

Explaining today's diversity of life is a bit mind-boggling. Since organisms appeared on Earth there've been a fair few barriers to population movement (e.g. mountains forming, continents splitting, sea level rises cutting islands in half), so it's not surprising that speciation has happened so many times. It's been estimated there could be up to 50 million species out there.

Other Hominids

Hominids are members of the family Hominidae, which includes modern humans, their ancestors, and the great apes (e.g. chimps and gorillas). These next few pages are all about bipedal hominids (the ones adapted to walk on two legs) — this only includes modern humans and their ancestors.

The Hominid 'Family Tree' Shows Who We're Descended From

1) Today, **humans** are the only member of the Hominidae family (see p. 58) that are **bipedal**, but **evidence** of many other bipedal hominids has been found in the fossil record.

2) These hominids are studied to build up a picture of **human evolution**.

The diagram below shows a simplified **bipedal hominid 'family tree'**. There are **uncertainties** and **gaps** in the family tree though because evidence from the fossil record is **limited** — **not many** fossils have been **found** and some fossils are **incomplete** or **damaged**.

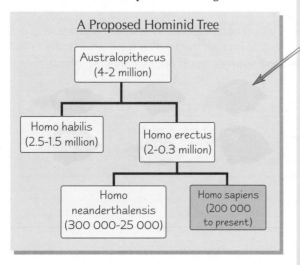

A Proposed Hominid Tree

Australopithecus (4-2 million)

Homo habilis (2.5-1.5 million)

Homo erectus (2-0.3 million)

Homo neanderthalensis (300 000-25 000)

Homo sapiens (200 000 to present)

Australopithecus (lived 4 - 2 million years ago)
They were **small** (1 - 1.5 m), with long arms and short legs, and brains roughly **35%** the size of a modern human brain. They're thought to be the **ancestors** of the genus *Homo*.

Homo habilis (lived 2.5 - 1.5 million years ago)
Habilis was the **same size** as *Australopithecus* but had a **larger brain** and **less protruding jaw**.

Homo erectus (lived 2 - 0.3 million years ago)
These were **taller** (around 1.8 m) and had a **larger brain** and even **less protruding jaw** than *habilis*.

Homo neanderthalensis (lived 300 000 - 25 000 years ago)
Neanderthals were of a similar height to *Homo sapiens* (about 1.7 m), with a **robust bone structure** and a **large brain**.

Homo sapiens (lived 200 000 years ago – present)
Modern humans have the **flattest jaw** and a **large brain**.

Human Ancestors had an Upright Posture

Fossils of bipedal hominids provide evidence for their ability to stand and walk upright:

1) Studying the **skeletal structure** of the knee, pelvis and spine can indicate whether upright walking was possible.

2) The **position** of the **hole** in the **skull** where the **spinal cord** exits can indicate whether a species had an upright posture.

3) Hominid **fossil footprints** that show bipedal walking have been found in 3.5 million year old volcanic ash.

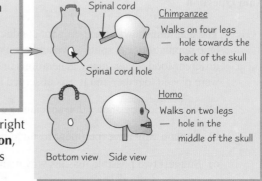

Chimpanzee
Walks on four legs — hole towards the back of the skull

Homo
Walks on two legs — hole in the middle of the skull

Bottom view   Side view

There are different theories about the selective advantage of walking upright — it leaves hands free to **carry** food or tools, increases the range of **vision**, enables **wading** in water, and is more **efficient** than walking on four legs over long distances.

The Cranial Capacity of Hominids has Increased Over Time

1) Hominid **fossil skulls** have been compared to see how **cranial size** has changed over time.

2) More modern hominids generally have a **larger cranial capacity**, which indicates a **larger brain size**.

3) The **evolution** of larger brains is considered important to hominid **evolution** — larger brains would be needed for the development and use of **tools**, complex **social relationships**, and **language** (see p. 68)

Other Hominids

Evidence of Diet Comes from Teeth, Bones and Tools

1) <u>Fossil teeth</u> — The **size**, **shape** and **wear** of fossil teeth can be studied.
   - *Australopithecus* ate mostly **plants** so had small canines and **big molars** for **grinding** plant matter.
   - They also had a **gap** (called a **diastema**) between their canines and incisors to allow food to **move** around more in the mouth.
   - As hominids started to eat **more meat** the **canines** and **incisors** **became sharper** for **tearing meat**, the molars became smaller and the diastema disappeared.

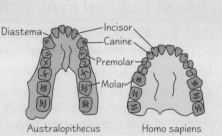

Australopithecus   Homo sapiens

2) <u>Bones</u> —
   - The **chemical composition** of hominid bones can indicate whether a species **ate** meat.
   - **Tool marks** on animal bones can provide evidence for **scraping**, **cutting** and **stabbing**, which in turn can provide evidence for **scavenging** and **hunting**.

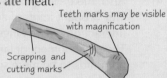

Teeth marks may be visible with magnification

Scrapping and cutting marks

3) <u>Tools</u> — Tools found with fossils provide evidence for **hunting** and **cutting** meat and bones (see p. 68).

Hominids evolved from vegetarians (who **scavenged** some meat) into **hunter-gatherers** (see p. 69):

Hominid	Diet	Evidence
Australopithecus	Mainly veg, possibly some meat	Heavy wear on teeth, analysis of bones suggests a small amount of meat eaten
Homo habilis	Veg with some meat	Simple tools for scraping and cracking bones
Homo erectus	Veg and meat	More complex tools for hunting
Homo neanderthalensis / sapiens	Veg and meat	Complex tools, evidence for hunter-gatherer lifestyle (see p. 69)

Interpreting Fossils can be Difficult

Fossils provide **limited** evidence — especially when they're **incomplete** or **damaged**.
It's also possible that scientists might **interpret** the fossil evidence differently. For example:

In 1932 an **incomplete lower jaw** of a hominid called *Ramapithecus* was found. Scientists thought the jaw and teeth were very **human-like**. They suggested that *Ramapithecus* was a **direct ancestor** of modern humans.

In 1975 and 1976 more **complete** fossils were found, which showed the jaw was **less human-like** than had initially been thought. *Ramapithecus* is no longer considered to be an ancestor of humans, and has been **reclassified** in a group with **orangutans**.

Practice Questions

Q1   Describe the trend in cranial capacity of hominids over time.

Q2   What is the evidence for hominids having an upright posture?

Exam Question

Q1   'Lucy' is a famous fossil hominid found in 1974. Her skeleton shows evidence of upright walking and is estimated to be 3.2 million years old.

   a) Suggest how scientists could use the fossil remains to find out about Lucy's diet.   [2 marks]

   b) Lucy is believed to be an ancestor of the genus *Homo*. Explain why there are different interpretations of how the genus *Homo* has evolved.   [2 marks]

If they looked at my teeth they'd not be pleased — chocolate, cake...

It's amazing what you can find out from looking at some really old fossils. It's important to remember that fossil evidence can be interpreted in different ways though — unlike the evidence, the ideas are not set in stone.

Cultural Evolution and Hunter-Gatherers

It was a slow process, but hominids gradually began to make and use tools, which became more and more complex.

Human *Cultural Evolution* Involved *Developing Tools* and *Controlling Fire*

1) Scientists study both the **physical evolution** of hominids (how their anatomy and physiology changed), and their **cultural evolution** (how their behaviour and social structures developed).

2) Physical and cultural evolution are often **linked**.

3) For example, the development of a **more complex brain** allowed hominids to **use tools** to hunt, which meant they could eat more meat. The **better diet** meant that they could develop **even larger** and **more complex brains**, which in turn enabled the development of **more complex tools**. And so on...

4) Also, the development of a **more complex brain** allowed hominids to **control fire**. This brought loads of advantages, e.g. providing a focal point for social interaction where **language** could develop and **knowledge** could be passed on. The development of language and the increase in knowledge-sharing allowed the hominids to be more successful in hunting, which improved the diet and led to the development of **even more complex brains**.

Sam's attempt to increase social interaction with a nice log fire had gone horribly wrong.

There's Plenty of Evidence for *Tool Use* and *Fire*

Archaeologists study the remains of tools and fires to figure out how they were **made** and what they were **used** for. This can be used to build up an idea of the **culture** of different **hominid species**. What we know about the evolution of tool and fire use is **limited** by the **quantity** and **quality** of the remains found so far. Evidence can be **dated** using **relative dating methods** and **radiometric dating** (see p. 63) of the **deposits** it's found in.

Evidence for **tool use** comes from:

1) **Actual tools** — the surfaces and edges of tools can be studied to identify **patterns of wear** or **residues** that might indicate how they were made or used.

2) **Artefacts** — objects that are found with tools, or around evidence of fires, can give clues about their use, e.g. oyster shells found near tools might suggest the tools were used to pry open the oyster shells to eat them.

3) **Experimental archaeology** — this can be used to test ideas and theories. It can involve making **similar tools** to see how they may have been made, e.g. making different flint tools and using them to cut animal bones.

Evidence for **controlling fire** comes from:

The remains of **hearths** (fireplaces). Some examples have been found and dated as **1.5 million years old**. Better evidence of hearths, along with supporting evidence such as fuel storage pits, have been dated as 60 000 years old.

Evidence is Used to Understand the Development of *Hominid Species*

Evidence of tools, controlling fire and art work (paintings and jewellery) has been used to determine the **cultural development** of the different hominid species.

Homo species	Cultural Evidence	
Homo habilis (2.5-1.5 million years ago)	Made simple stone tools by hitting rocks together. The sharp flakes obtained could be used for scraping meat from bones and cracking open bones. Sometimes called pebble tools.	Pebble tool
Homo erectus (2-0.3 million years ago)	Moved from pebble tools to sculpting rocks into shapes to produce more complex tools like simple hand-axes. Could be used to hunt, dig, chop and scrape meat from bones. First evidence of controlled use of fire.	Simple hand-axe
Homo neanderthalensis (300 000-25 000 years ago)	More complex tools and controlled use of fire. Evidence of flint tools, pointed tools and wooden spears.	
Homo sapiens (200 000 - present)	Controlled use of fire. Flint tools widely used. Pointed tools including arrowheads, fish-hooks, buttons and needles appeared around 50 000 years ago. First evidence of art.	Arrow tip

Cultural Evolution and Hunter-Gatherers

Early Humans *Lived in a* Hunter-Gatherer *Society*

Some hominids began living in **hunter-gatherer** societies around 2 million years ago. Hunter-gatherers **collect** wild plants and **hunt** wild animals. What we know about their societies comes from **archaeological evidence** and studies of historical and **living** hunter-gatherers, e.g. the Maasai tribe in Africa.

Early Humans Lived Together in Small Groups...

Groups of hunter-gatherers typically contained **10-30 individuals**, although these smaller groups might have interacted with each other and gathered food together when it was abundant. The size of a group would have been determined by the **resources** available — if a group became too large to be supported by the local food sources, some of the individuals would have left to establish a new group elsewhere.

...Made Up of One or More Families

Hunter-gatherers probably existed in **family groups** made up of children, parents, grandparents and other extended family members. It's likely that the men and women were mostly **monogamous** (one man mated with one woman), and shared the responsibility of caring for their children. Grandparents probably had an important role in passing on their **knowledge** and **skills**, and helping to care for the children.

They Moved Around but had a Home Base

The group would have had a **home base** (a settlement) which offered shelter, warmth from a fire and cooking facilities. Individuals would have hunted and gathered in a **range** about their home base. A settlement might be **permanent**, **temporary** or **seasonal**. Hunter-gatherers often moved their settlements in search of food (for example, a tribe might move to follow the migration of wildebeest).

Different People in the Group had Different Roles

It's likely that individuals in the group would have had different **roles** and **responsibilities** — hunting, gathering, preparing and cooking food, making tools and caring for children may have been done by different individuals. There is evidence of a **sexual division of labour** in many societies (the men hunted and the woman gathered wild fruits and vegetables) — but there are exceptions to this pattern.

Groups were Cooperative

One of the key features of hunter-gatherer societies was **cooperation**. Individuals **worked together** to gather resources. Cooperation has many benefits — hunting together enables **larger prey** to be caught, and living together enables individuals to **learn** from each other and **share** food and responsibilities. Complex **social interactions** and systems of values and beliefs are thought to have evolved in hunter-gatherer societies.

Practice Questions

Q1 Which species of hominid used only pebble tools?

Q2 Suggest two benefits of being able to control fire.

Exam Question

Q1 Excavations in France have revealed evidence of basic shelters constructed around 150 000 years ago. Stone tools and fragments of animal bones were found surrounding two circular charcoal concentrations, which may have been hearths.

a) Suggest what the stone tools might have been used for, giving a reason for your answer. [2 marks]

b) Scientists have suggested that the cave was used by a group of early hunter-gatherers. Describe the characteristics of hunter-gatherer societies. [7 marks]

Did you notice — not a single gag about Homo erectus...

Over two million years, the tools that hominids made became much more complex. This suggests that the brains of these species were also becoming more complex. At first, just the sharp flakes chipped off stones were used as tools. Gradually, species developed the skills to be able to create a specific shape (e.g. an arrowhead) from a piece of stone.

Anatomical and Behavioural Adaptations

If we weren't adapted to our environment, we'd struggle to survive. But, luckily, we are...

Humans are **Adapted** to Their **Environment**

Being **adapted** to our environment means we have features that **increase** our **chances of survival** and **reproduction**, and also the chances of our **children reproducing successfully**. These features are called **adaptations** and can be:

1) **Anatomical** — structural features
2) **Behavioural** — the way we act
3) **Physiological** — how the body works

Karen wasn't as structurally adapted to hiding behind lamp posts as she thought.

Humans have developed these adaptations by **natural selection** (see p. 60).
In each generation, the **best-adapted individuals** are more likely to survive and reproduce — passing their adaptations on to their **offspring**. Individuals that are less well adapted are more likely to **die before reproducing**.

Humans Have **Anatomical Adaptations**

Make sure you know the following examples:

Bipedalism (walking on two feet)

1) By standing on two feet, the **head** is **raised** and the **eyes** are **higher**. This allowed our ancestors to see over **obstacles**, which was useful for **finding food** and **spotting predators** a long way off.
2) Bipedalism also **freed up** the **hands** for other things — like **tool use**.
3) So, bipedalism allowed our ancestors to find **more food** and **avoid predators more easily**, which increased their chances of **survival** and **reproduction**.

Opposable thumbs

1) This is where the **thumb** can be **pushed against the fingers**.
2) This adaptation allowed our ancestors to **manipulate tools**, helping them **hunt** and **build shelters**, which increased the chances of them **finding food** and **protected** them from **predators** and **harsh weather conditions**.
3) Both of these things increased their chances of **survival** and **reproduction**.

Humans have opposable thumbs, allowing a grip between thumb and fingers.

Skin colour

1) In humans, the main skin pigment (**melanin**) absorbs **UV radiation** from the Sun, **stopping** it from **damaging** the tissues underneath. The **darker** the skin, the **more** melanin and the **better** the UV protection.
2) But humans also need sunlight to synthesise **vitamin D**, and melanin **interferes with this process**.
3) Having **dark skin** in sunny places (e.g. Africa) is an **advantage** because **more melanin** protects you from UV radiation, but the **intensity** and **length** of daylight still allows the production of enough **vitamin D**.
4) When humans migrated out of Africa to **less sunny** parts of the world, their dark skin affected their **ability to synthesise vitamin D** because the Sun was **less intense** and the **number** of daylight hours was lower. The skin colour of these humans gradually became **paler** due to a **reduction** in melanin.
5) This was an advantage in these areas because **less melanin** allowed the production of enough **vitamin D** but was still enough to protect the skin from the **less intense UV radiation** in these areas.

Surface area to volume ratio

1) This ratio **compares** the size of an organism's **surface area** to its **volume**. Different ethnic groups have different ratios because they're adapted to **different climates**. The **typical body shapes** of an African tribesman and an Inuit from the Arctic are pretty different.
2) In a **hot climate**, a **long-limbed** body shape gives a **larger surface area to volume ratio** so it's easier to **lose body heat** (increasing survival). But in a **cold climate**, a more **compact** body shape **decreases** the **surface area to volume ratio** and helps to **keep heat in** (also increasing survival).

Anatomical and Behavioural Adaptations

Behavioural and Sociological Adaptations Increase the Chance of Survival

In humans, **behavioural** and **sociological** adaptations are important.

1) **Behavioural adaptations** are **ways we act** that make it more likely that we'll **survive** and **reproduce**. For example, we learn to **repeat** actions that bring us **rewards**, like food, which makes it more likely that we'll be able to get those rewards again.

2) **Sociological adaptations** are ways that members of a **group interact** that improve the survival chances of the whole group. or example, people can **communicate** to warn each other of danger.

Behavioural and sociological adaptations include:

1) **Communication** using **facial expressions**. Many of these, like smiling, frowning and blushing, are **innate** (inborn) reactions. Communication using facial expressions helps people know what others are **thinking** or **feeling**. This helps them **cooperate** when doing things like hunting, growing food, avoiding predators and raising young. So, facial expressions make **survival** and **reproduction** more likely.

2) The development of **language** during childhood. This improves **survival** chances as it allows the young to **communicate** their **needs** to their parents — much better than just using facial expressions.

3) **Extended childhood.** A long childhood allows children to **learn** more from their parents. **Knowledge** and **culture** can be passed on to the next generation, so they're more likely to survive in their environment. (One disadvantage is that the young are fairly **helpless** for a long time.)

Make Sure You Can Suggest How an Adaptation Contributes to Survival

In the exam you could be asked **how an adaptation helps survival**. The sorts of things you need to consider are:

1) Does the adaptation help in **avoiding predators**? E.g. being able to hide, running away.
2) Does it help in **defending** against predators or parasites? E.g. big horns.
3) Does it help in surviving **difficult conditions**? E.g. waterproof skin.
4) Does it help to get **food**? E.g. using tools.
5) Does it help in **reproduction**? E.g. attracting a mate.

For example, another behavioural characteristic of humans is **using fire** (see p. 68). It's a special adaptation because it's only found in **our species**. It increases our survival in many ways — frightening off **predators**, keeping **warm** and **cooking** food.

Practice Questions

Q1 Why do natives of Siberia have a relatively low surface area to volume ratio?
Q2 Explain the difference between behavioural and sociological adaptations.
Q3 Why is communicating through facial expressions a useful adaptation?

Exam Question

Q1 One human anatomical adaptation is bipedalism.

a) What is meant by bipedalism? [1 mark]

b) Explain two advantages of bipedalism in humans. [2 marks]

c) Opposable thumbs and paler skin colour are two other human anatomical adaptations. Describe how they contribute to survival. [2 marks]

Opposable thumbs — they're really disagreeable...

We're not only adapted anatomically — we're also adapted in the way we behave. I know there's quite a few of them, but make sure you know how all the adaptations on these pages increased survival. In the exam, be prepared to be asked about an adaptation that you might not have come across before — just think carefully about why it's a useful trait to have.

Physiological Adaptations

As well as structural and behavioural adaptations, we also have physiological adaptations. These are processes inside the body that've developed to cope with different situations, e.g. if I was running a marathon my heart rate and breathing rate would increase to supply my muscles with enough glucose and oxygen to keep me going. Me... a marathon... as if.

Physiological Adaptations are Advantageous

Physiological adaptations are **processes** in the body that increase the chances of survival. They allow us to cope with different situations, e.g. **vigorous exercise**. The body is adapted to cope with vigorous exercise by:

1) **Increasing breathing rate** — to obtain more **oxygen** and to get rid of more **carbon dioxide**.

2) **Increasing heart rate** — to **deliver oxygen** (and glucose) to the muscles **faster** and **remove** extra carbon dioxide produced by **respiration** in muscle cells.

3) **Changing the energy source used by muscles** — to provide enough energy for respiration if one energy source runs low.

The fact that the body can respond to vigorous exercise is an **advantage** — it makes us **more efficient** at catching prey, escaping danger, etc. It also means that we **don't waste resources** when we're at rest, e.g. taking in more oxygen than we need.

The *Medulla* and *Stretch Receptors Control Breathing Rate*

The **ventilation cycle** is the cycle of breathing in and out. It involves **inspiratory** and **expiratory** centres in the **medulla** (an area of the **brain**) and **stretch receptors** in the **lungs**.

1) The **inspiratory centre** in the **medulla** sends nerve impulses to the **intercostal** and **diaphragm** muscles (see p. 20) to make them **contract**. This lowers the pressure in the lungs. The inspiratory centre also sends nerve impulses to the **expiratory centre**. These impulses **inhibit** the action of the **expiratory centre**.

2) Air enters the lungs due to the **pressure difference** between the lungs and the air outside.

3) As the **lungs inflate**, **stretch receptors** in the lungs are **stimulated**. The stretch receptors send nerve impulses back to the **medulla**. These impulses **inhibit** the action of the **inspiratory centre**.

4) The expiratory centre (no longer inhibited) then sends nerve impulses to the **diaphragm** and **intercostal muscles** to **relax**. This causes the **lungs to deflate**, expelling air. As the lungs deflate, the **stretch receptors** become **inactive**. The inspiratory centre is no longer inhibited and the cycle starts again.

5) This ventilation cycle happens **automatically**, without you having to think about it.

Breathing Rate Increases Due to Increased Muscular Activity

The **more** your muscles contract, the **more energy** they use. To replace this energy your body needs to do more **aerobic respiration**, so it needs to take in more **oxygen** and breathe out more **carbon dioxide**. The body can do this by **increasing the breathing rate** — a physiological adaptation that helps us cope with exercise. Here's how it works:

1) During exercise, **carbon dioxide** (CO_2) levels rise. This **decreases** the **pH** of the blood.

2) There are **chemoreceptors** (receptors that sense chemicals) in the **medulla**, **aortic bodies** (in the aorta) and **carotid bodies** (in the carotid arteries carrying blood to the brain) that are **sensitive** to changes in blood pH.

3) If the chemoreceptors **detect** a **decrease** in the **pH** of the blood, they send a **signal** to the **medulla** to send **more frequent** nerve impulses to the **intercostal muscles** and **diaphragm**. This **increases** the **rate** and **depth** of breathing.

4) This causes **gaseous exchange** to **speed up** — CO_2 levels drop and extra O_2 is supplied for the muscles.

The *Medulla Controls Heart Rate*

Heart rate is **controlled** by the **cardiovascular centre** in the **medulla** of the brain. **Nerve impulses** are sent from the cardiac centre to the **SAN** (see p. 38). These nerve impulses **speed up** or **slow down** our heart rate.

Physiological Adaptations

Heart Rate Increases *Due to* Increased Muscular Activity

Increased muscular activity causes **decreased blood pH** (due to the extra CO_2 produced — see previous page) and **increased blood pressure**. In addition to the breathing rate, the **heart rate changes** to compensate for this — another **physiological adaptation** to exercise. Here's how it works:

Decreased blood pH causes an increase in heart rate

1) A decrease in **blood pH** is detected by **chemoreceptors**.

2) The chemoreceptors send **nerve impulses** to the brain.

3) The brain sends its own nerve impulses to the SAN to **increase the heart rate**.

Increased blood pressure causes a decrease in heart rate

1) **Pressure receptors** in the **aorta wall** and in the **carotid sinuses** (at the start of the carotid arteries carrying blood to the brain) **detect changes** in **arterial blood pressure** and inform the brain.

2) If the pressure is **too high**, pressure receptors send **nerve impulses** to the cardiovascular centre. This sends nerve impulses to the **SAN**, to **slow down the heart rate**.

3) If the **pressure is too low**, pressure receptors send nerve impulses to the cardiovascular centre, which sends its own nerve impulses to, yep you guessed it, the SAN, to **speed up** the **heart rate**.

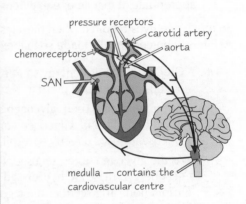

Cardiac Output Increases *with* Exercise

1) Cardiac output is the **total volume** of blood pumped by a **ventricle** every **minute**.

2) It gives a good **indication** of how **effective** the delivery of blood (and therefore oxygen) to respiring cells is.

3) When you're **exercising**, your muscle cells need **more oxygen**, so cardiac output **increases** to supply this demand.

> Stroke volume is the **volume** of blood **pumped** by one **ventricle** each time it **contracts**.

4) You need to learn the equation:

> **Cardiac output** (cm^3/min) = **heart rate** (beats per minute) × **stroke volume** (cm^3)

Practice Questions

Q1 Which part of the brain controls the breathing rate and heart rate?

Q2 What effect does exercise have on cardiac output?

Exam Question

Q1 In a laboratory experiment, an animal was anaesthetised and dilute carbonic acid (carbon dioxide in solution) was added to the blood in the coronary artery.

a) What effect would you expect this to have on the animal's breathing rate? Explain your answer. [5 marks]

b) Cardiac output increased in response to the addition of carbonic acid.
How is cardiac output calculated? [1 mark]

My cat has a huge stroke volume — it could sit there being petted all day...

Breathing rate and heart rate can be increased to supply more oxygen for aerobic respiration, which produces the energy the body needs in certain situations. Another physiological adaptation is having a specialised gut that can break down many different types of food molecules (e.g. proteins, fats, carbohydrates). These adaptations help us to survive.

Physiological Adaptations

Each physiological adaptation has evolved because it gives us an advantage. Being adapted to cope with vigorous exercise helps us to catch prey, avoid predators etc. So, just for you, here are some more adaptations...

We're Adapted to Use Different **Energy Sources** During **Exercise**

1) Muscles **need energy** to **contract**.

2) This energy comes from the **breakdown** of a molecule called **ATP** — it's the **immediate energy source**.

3) ATP is **produced** by the **breakdown** of other **energy sources** (such as **glucose**, **glycogen** and **fats**) in **respiration**.

4) The energy sources have **different properties**. E.g. **glucose** is **easily transported** in the blood, which is perfect for a **quick energy source**, whereas **fat** is **insoluble** so it's an ideal energy source for **long-term storage**.

5) It's an advantage for cells to be able to **change** their energy source — they can use the source that's most appropriate at that time, e.g. glucose after dinner, fat after a period of **food shortage**.

So much energy is required when muscles contract that the available ATP gets **used up quickly**. ATP has to be **continually made** so that exercise can carry on.

1) **Glucose** is the first energy source to be used. This is found in the cytoplasm of cells and in blood plasma.

2) As the glucose is used, **glycogen** stores in the **liver** and **muscles** are broken down to replace it. Glycogen can easily be **hydrolysed** (see p. 12) into glucose, or used directly in respiration.

3) As the glycogen stores get used, the body breaks down **triglycerides** (fats) to get energy. These are **hydrolysed** to **fatty acids** and **glycerol** and used in respiration. Triglycerides are a good **long-term energy store** because they have **lots of energy per gram** — about twice as much as glucose or glycogen.

The aches from exercise ease quickly but the shame of that outfit will last a lifetime.

Respiration can be **Aerobic** or **Anaerobic**

There are **two different types** of respiration — **aerobic** and **anaerobic**. Aerobic respiration takes place when we can take in **plenty of oxygen**, e.g. at rest. When aerobic respiration can't keep up with the demand for oxygen, e.g. during vigorous exercise, anaerobic respiration takes place **as well**.

Aerobic Respiration

1) It **uses oxygen** and **produces** CO_2, which is breathed out.

2) It releases **more energy** from each glucose molecule than anaerobic respiration (so makes **more ATP**).

Anaerobic Respiration

1) It **doesn't** need **oxygen** to release energy.

2) Anaerobic respiration **produces lactate**, which **builds up** in the **blood**. It also **lowers the blood pH**, which causes the pain known as **muscle fatigue**.

3) It's **less efficient** at releasing energy than aerobic respiration (so doesn't make as much ATP).

Lactate is formed when lactic acid loses a H^+ ion.

The **Lactate** Produced in **Anaerobic** Respiration has to be **Broken Down**

During **vigorous exercise** the body needs more oxygen than is available, so it starts to respire anaerobically.

1) The **lactate** that's produced is **toxic** — the body can only deal with it in **small amounts**.

2) When exercise stops, **oxygen** is needed to **get rid** of the lactate.

3) The amount of oxygen needed to remove lactate is called the **oxygen debt**. This is why you keep **panting** after hard exercise — you're still **repaying** the oxygen debt.

4) Some lactate is **broken down** in the **muscles** and some is carried to the **liver** where it's changed into **glucose** and **stored** as glycogen.

Physiological Adaptations

Humans are **Adapted** to Adjust to **High Altitude**

1) As altitude **increases**, air pressure **decreases** — air becomes **thinner**.

2) This means that, in a given volume of air, there are **fewer molecules**. The composition of the air stays the same (there's still 21% oxygen) — there's just fewer molecules of everything. So, you'd inhale fewer oxygen molecules standing on top of Everest than you would at sea level.

3) People who live at high altitudes have **more red blood cells** than people who live at lower altitudes because humans have an adaptation that allows them to increase the number of red blood cells when oxygen is low. (If you moved to a high altitude your body would produce more red blood cells.)

Even though Sayeed had only climbed up 10 metres he could feel his red blood cells increasing.

4) More red blood cells means there's **more haemoglobin** (see below) to carry oxygen. This means the blood can **physically carry** more oxygen and supply more oxygen to the muscles.

> 1) Oxygen is carried round the body in red blood cells by a **protein** called **haemoglobin** (Hb).
>
> 2) Oxygen **joins** to haemoglobin in the lungs to form **oxyhaemoglobin**.
>
> 3) This is a **reversible reaction** — when oxygen leaves oxyhaemoglobin (dissociates from it) near the body cells, it turns back to haemoglobin.
>
> $$Hb \quad + \quad 4O_2 \quad \rightleftharpoons \quad HbO_8$$
> haemoglobin + oxygen $\rightleftharpoons$ oxyhaemoglobin
>
> *Each haemoglobin molecule can carry four oxygen molecules.*

You Need to be Able to Figure Out **How Adaptations Improve Survival**

In the exam, you could be given an example of a physiological adaptation that you **haven't studied** and be asked to suggest how it **helps survival**. Don't panic — just use your common sense.

For example, does the adaptation:

> 1) **Maintain a condition** in the body? E.g. body temperature, breathing rate, heart rate.
>
> 2) Help in the production of **energy**? E.g. long-term sources of energy.
>
> 3) Enable someone to live in a certain **environment**? E.g. at high altitude.

Practice Questions

Q1 Name three different energy sources we can use during prolonged exercise.

Q2 Describe an adaptation we have to living at high altitudes.

Exam Question

Q1 The concentration of lactate in an athlete's blood was measured before, during and after exercise.

a) What process in the body produces blood lactate? [1 mark]

b) Give one advantage and one disadvantage of this process. [2 marks]

c) Describe what will happen to the concentration of lactate in the athlete's blood after he finishes exercising. Explain your answer. [2 marks]

Maple syrup — my favourite energy source...

By now, you've probably begun to realise how important it is for us to have the adaptations that we have. Without them, we'd be pretty much stuffed. For example, if you wanted to live at high altitude (e.g. you fancied yourself as a Tibetan yak herder) you couldn't because you wouldn't be able to get enough oxygen from the thin air without adapting.

Parasite Adaptations

Parasites are adapted to live in or on other organisms. It's alright for some — parasites get free shelter and food.

Parasites depend on a Host to Survive

Parasites are organisms that **live in** or **on** another organism (the host), **feeding** on it and **causing damage**.

1) Some parasites live on the **surface** of their host, e.g. fleas.
2) Some live in the **gut**, e.g. tapeworms.
3) Some live in the **blood** or other parts of the body, e.g. the malarial parasite.

Parasites are Adapted to Their Environment and Way of Life

Most parasites are **sheltered** from the outside world and their **food** is readily available. But parasites have to be able to **survive** inside a host and infect new hosts — they do this through a number of **adaptations**.

① **Adaptations to survive inside a host**

The inside of a host can be quite a **hostile environment** — the body is constantly trying to kill or remove the parasites. A successful parasite must be adapted to survive host protection mechanisms. Adaptations to protect themselves against **digestive enzymes** include:

- **Thick outer coverings** — e.g. tapeworms have a **cuticle** to protect themselves from digestion.
- **Anti-enzymes** — e.g. roundworms and tapeworms produce substances that inhibit digestive enzymes.

Adaptations to protect themselves against the **immune system** include:

- **Antigenic variation** — the parasite continually changes its **surface antigens** (see p. 32), so the immune system never quite catches up. E.g. the parasite that causes malaria does this.
- **Living inside host cells** — the antibodies of the immune system can't **reach them**. E.g. viruses do this.
- **Surface coatings** — E.g. pneumonia bacteria may have a **capsule** to protect them from phagocytes.

Adaptations to stay inside the host and **obtain food**:

- **Anatomical adaptations** — E.g. the hookworm has **hooks** (unsurprisingly) which it uses to hang on to the gut wall. Insects like lice and fleas have **piercing mouthparts** to suck blood.

② **Adaptations to increase infection of a new host**

Most offspring produced by parasites **die** or don't successfully **infect** new hosts.
Parasites have adapted to try to increase the chance of their offspring being successful by:

- **Producing lots of offspring** — more offspring means more are likely to survive and successfully infect a new host. E.g. one tapeworm can produce over 50 million fertilised eggs a year.
- **Using secondary hosts for transmission** — some parasites have adapted to infect a **secondary host**. Usually they only live in this organism for a short time and they use them to **infect new hosts**. E.g. **malaria** parasites use **mosquitoes** as **secondary hosts**. An infected **human host** is bitten by a mosquito, which takes up blood containing the **parasites**. In the mosquito, the parasites **replicate** and travel to the **salivary gland**. The mosquito bites a new human and the parasites **pass** into the bloodstream, infecting a **new host**.

Some Parasites Have Reduced Organ Systems

Some parasites have adapted to living inside a host by reducing the **number of organs** they have. This means they don't **waste energy** on organs and organ **processes** that **aren't needed** inside a host. Here are some examples:

1) **No locomotion organs** — parasites inside a host **don't need to move** to look for food. E.g. parasitic flatworms (like tapeworms and liver flukes) can't move much — they lack **developed muscles** and **cilia**.

2) **No digestive system** — a parasite's food is ready-digested inside a host. E.g. tapeworms have no **gut** — they **absorb** nutrients from digested food.

3) **No nervous system** and **reduced sense organs** — parasites inside the body don't need **eyes**, and they have little information to **process** and don't need to **control movement**.

Yoga move 15: the parasite.

Parasite Adaptations

Toxocara is a *Parasite* that *infects Animals* (and *Humans*)

Some parasites that normally infect **other animals** can sometimes **infect humans**.

1) *Toxocara* is a roundworm. It normally infects **dogs** and **cats**, living in their gut. Apart from **stealing food** it doesn't do that much harm to the host animal.

2) *Toxocara* can also **infect humans** — the infection is called **toxocariasis**. It can make people **ill** and can even cause **blindness** if the infection gets into the eyes.

3) The **faeces** of an **infected animal** contain the **parasite eggs**. These are tiny and can remain in the soil for a long time. People can be infected when they **touch contaminated soil** or if they **handle a contaminated animal**, and then put their hands in their **mouth** or **eyes**.

4) The **risk of infection** of people is increased when dogs **poo** in **public places**, like parks. **Young children** are especially **vulnerable** as they are more likely to **crawl** on the ground and put **unwashed fingers** in their mouths.

The *toxocara* parasite is well-adapted for its parasitic life because:

1) It produces **large numbers** of eggs, for the best chance of infecting a new host.

2) It has a **cuticle**, to resist **digestion** by the host's digestive enzymes.

3) The larvae secrete thick **mucus**, which protects them against the host's **immune system**.

4) The eggs have a **strong shell** and can stay **dormant** (inactive) for years.

5) The eggs are **sticky**, which helps them to infect animals.

You Might have to Evaluate Parasite Adaptations in the *Exam*

In the exam, you might be told about a **parasite** that you **haven't seen before** and then asked to say **how** it's **adapted** to its **environment**. Remember to think about these **features** and you should be fine:

1) How does the parasite **protect** itself against its host? E.g. it has a thick protective cuticle or other covering, which protects it from being digested by enzymes.

2) How does it **attach** itself to the host? E.g. hooks, claws or suckers.

3) How does it **transfer** from one host to another? E.g. life-cycle adaptations such as a second host, or production of resistant eggs.

4) What's special about its way of **reproducing**? E.g. rapid rate of reproduction.

5) Does it have any **reduced structures**? E.g. sense organs, nervous system and gut.

Shelter... food... Joanne suddenly realised that her children were a type of parasite that she hadn't considered before.

Practice Questions

Q1   What is a parasite?

Q2   Give five ways that parasites are often adapted to their way of life.

Exam Question

Q1   The photo shows part of a tapeworm. This is a parasite that lives in the human gut.

a) Suggest the function of the structure labelled X. [1 mark]

b) The tapeworm has no digestive system. Explain why this is not necessary. [1 mark]

c) Suggest one reproductive adaptation that the tapeworm might have. Explain why this adaptation is beneficial to the tapeworm. [2 marks]

STEVE GSCHMEISSNER / SCIENCE PHOTO LIBRARY

X

Parasites often don't have eyes — so that's parastes then...

Parasites — the cheek of them. They move in and use our bodies as shelter and then steal our food. And without even asking first... pah. So, as you've probably gathered, they're pretty nasty things. They've got loads of adaptations too — some of which help them to survive our immune system's best efforts to get rid of them. Evil geniuses...

Impact of Farming on the Landscape

Farming began changing our environment around 11 000 years ago — that's a long time of putting up with pongy cow smells...

Evidence Shows that Humans First Began Farming About 10 000 Years Ago

Archaeological evidence suggests that the change from a **nomadic hunter-gatherer** way of life (see p. 69) to **farming** started in several places independently about 10 000 to 12 000 years ago — although some hunter-gatherer societies still exist today. The **archaeological evidence** for early farming includes:

1) **The remains of settlements** — farming settlements have characteristic features such as crop growing areas and storage facilities.

2) **Farming tools** — for example, sowing and harvesting tools.

3) **The remains of seed stores** — of the first domesticated plants (like wheat and barley).

4) **Evidence of domesticated animals** — for example, animal remains and holding pens.

5) **Artwork** — showing farming practices.

Tina (right) had managed
to hold a fork but hadn't
quite grasped holding pens.

Farming has Changed the Landscape and Ecosystems of the UK

Farming dramatically changes the natural environment. Both the **landscape** (the visible features of the land) and the **ecosystems** (the organisms and the physical factors in an area) of the UK are the result of farming practices.

Woodland was Chopped Down

Before farming, the UK was mostly covered by **dense woodland**. When farming began, woodland was cleared to **make room** for farming **settlements**, **arable** (crop-growing) land and land for animals to **graze** on. The process of clearing woodland is called **deforestation**. It affects the natural environment in many ways:

1) It **reduces biodiversity** because habitats are lost.

2) It **changes local weather systems** — rainfall and humidity are reduced.

3) It **increases soil erosion** and reduces **soil quality**.

Biodiversity is the variation of life forms. See page 81 for more information.

The first areas to be cleared for farming were in **southern Britain**. The land that had been cleared was only suitable for growing crops for a **few years**. After this, the **soil quality** wasn't good enough so more land had to be cleared. This process was repeated over many years. It led to the creation of huge **open areas** of **heathland** — areas with poor quality soil and low growing vegetation.

Wetland was Drained

It wasn't just woodland that changed. **Wetlands** (areas with saturated soils such as swamps and marshes) were **drained** to make them suitable for farming. Just like deforestation, this reduced biodiversity and changed the landscape.

Example: The New Forest

The **New Forest** is an area of **southern England** that includes forest, heathland and wetland.

1) Just like the rest of the UK, the New Forest was mostly **dense woodland** before farming began.

2) Early farmers **cleared** areas of woodland and farmed them until the **soil quality** became too poor.

3) Gradually the landscape changed — the woodland became replaced by **arable** and **grazing** fields, **settlements** and **heathland**.

4) In the 11th century, the areas of forest that remained were declared a **royal hunting ground** and as a result large areas of the forest have been **preserved** to this day.

Impact of Farming on the Landscape

You may have to **Evaluate Evidence** about **Changes** to the **Landscape**

In the exam, you could be asked to **evaluate** the influence human activities have had on the landscape. Here's an example of the kind of evidence you might get:

The diagram below shows a section of **peat**. Studies of **pollen** preserved in peat can provide evidence about how the **vegetation** has **changed** in an area.

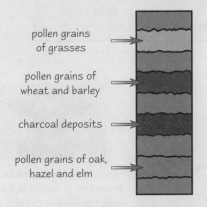

pollen grains of grasses

pollen grains of wheat and barley

charcoal deposits

pollen grains of oak, hazel and elm

1) The **oldest** pollen grains are found at the **bottom** of the core. Oak, hazel and elm indicate a **woodland** environment.

2) The **charcoal** deposits above are the result of **burning**. Early farming communities often used **fire** to **clear woodland** to make room for fields and settlements.

3) Pollen grains of **wheat** and **barley** above the charcoal are evidence of **arable farming**.

4) The **grass pollen** found at the top of the core indicates that the land was no longer being used for crops. The land could have been used for **grazing**, or **not farmed** at all.

The changes in vegetation shown by the core are likely to be the result of **farming activities**. However, other explanations, like a change in **climate**, should also be considered. Further evidence that would support the theory that farming changed the vegetation in this area would include **archaeological evidence** like the remains of settlements, farming tools, and fences or field boundaries.

Practice Questions

Q1 Roughly when did humans begin farming?

Q2 Give five examples of evidence for early arable farming.

Q3 Why did the development of farming lead to deforestation?

Q4 Why was wetland in the UK drained?

Exam Question

Q1 The archaeological excavation of a 4000-year-old settlement revealed the remains of several buildings and numerous artefacts such as tools and pottery. From the evidence gathered, scientists thought that the settlement was a pig farm.

a) Suggest two pieces of evidence that archaeologists might have found that would indicate that the settlement was a pig farm. [2 marks]

b) Describe three ways in which the landscape and ecosystem of the surrounding area could have been affected by a developing farming community. [3 marks]

c) A scientist studying the remains of insects in sediment near the excavation found that there was a drop in the number of insect species in deposits the same age as the settlement. Suggest an explanation for this finding. [2 marks]

Evidence of farming — fossilised cow pats...

In the exam, you might have to interpret some evidence about how us humans have affected the landscape. Don't panic — just use your common sense and you'll be fine. Be careful what you conclude from the data though — don't go saying that the changes were definitely caused by farming (there could be plenty of other reasons).

Farming Practices and Impact on Biodivesity

The hunter-gatherer lifestyle became a bit old hat as more and more people were seduced by the promise of being farmers (yes, farming is seductive to some people)... well, who wouldn't want to raise animals and grow crops all day?

Farming Involves the Cultivation of Crops and Domestication of Animals

Cultivation of Crops

Some of the first crops to be cultivated were plants with **edible seeds**, like wheat, barley, peas, lentils, chickpeas and rice. These plants are **easy to grow**, they produce seeds that are easy to **store**, and they grow **quickly** — providing a more reliable source of food than gathering wild plants.

Domestication of Animals

Domestication is where animals become used to being **provided for** and **controlled** by humans. Animals have been domesticated over generations, gradually becoming more **docile** and **easier to handle**. Humans domesticated animals to produce **food** and **other materials** (such as wool or leather), to **help us** (e.g. by providing transport or protection) and to enjoy as **pets**. Animals that grew quickly, could breed in captivity, could be fed easily and had a suitable disposition (not too aggressive) were domesticated. The first animals to be domesticated included **dogs**, **goats**, **cats**, **sheep**, **pigs**, **cows** and **chickens**.

Elsie was pleased to be getting a promotion — until she learnt it was from pulling the plough to becoming finest beef...

Growing Crops and Raising Animals Led to Larger Settlements

1) The change from hunting and gathering to farming meant that communities began to build **permanent settlements** around their crops and domesticated animals.

2) Farming not only produced **more food** from an area than could be obtained by hunting and gathering, but it also provided a much **more reliable food source** — this led to a **food surplus**.

3) The food surplus meant that the **size** of farming settlements **grew**. It supported an **increase** in both **population size** and **population density** (the population size per unit area).

Selective Breeding Produced Useful Features in Cereals, Dogs and Cattle

Selective breeding involves choosing individuals with **desirable characteristics** from a population of plants or animals, then breeding them. Over generations this leads to **changes in the population**, making the organisms more useful to us.

There are loads of everyday examples:

1) Many **cereals** have been selectively bred — including rye, maize, rice, wheat, barley and oats. Useful characteristics that have been selected for include **high germination rates**, **high yields**, **resistance to disease** and **resistance to frost**.

2) **Dogs** have been selectively bred since they were domesticated from wolves over 15 000 years ago. The **characteristics** that are selected for in dogs (like **size**, **appearance** and **temperament**) depend on what the dog is **used** for. A hunting dog will have very different characteristics from a herding dog or a pet. As a result many different **breeds** of dog exist today that show a great variation in size, appearance and behaviour.

3) **Cattle** were domesticated around 10 000 years ago. They were used to pull **carts** and **ploughs** and to provide **meat**, **dairy products** and **leather**. Selective breeding has created a range of **breeds** suitable for these uses. For example, some breeds produce lots of meat and others produce lots of milk.

Farming Practices and Impact on Biodivesity

Human Activities can have an Impact on Biodiversity

Biodiversity is the **variation** of organisms in an area. There are different levels of biodiversity, and human activity affects them in various ways.

1) The **genetic diversity** within a species — for example, selective breeding affects the genetic diversity of a species (usually reducing it).

2) The **number of different species** in an ecosystem — for example, growing crops in place of woodland decreases the diversity of plant species in some areas.

3) The **number of different ecosystems** in an area — for example, draining wetlands to create farmland has reduced the diversity of ecosystems in some areas.

In the exam, you might be asked to evaluate the impact of **human activities** (like farming) on **biodiversity** and the **environment**. For example:

In 1950, the fields on Overend farm were separated by **hedgerows**. In 1960, the hedgerows were **removed** to give a **larger field area** and to make the **sowing** and **harvesting** of crops **easier**. In 1994, the hedgerows were **replanted** to try to **increase biodiversity** in the area. The graph below shows the numbers of bird and mammal species recorded on Overend farm in 1950, 1990 and 2000.

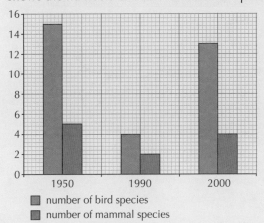

- number of bird species
- number of mammal species

1) The graph shows that when there **were hedgerows** on the farm (1950 and 2000) there was a much **greater diversity** of bird and mammal species than when there were no hedgerows (1990).

2) This is because hedgerows provide **habitat**, **shelter** and **food** for birds and mammals. They also act as **wildlife corridors**, linking areas of woodland and enabling animals to move between them safely.

3) The loss of the hedgerows would also have reduced **plant diversity**, **insect diversity** and **overall biodiversity** on the farm.

Practice Questions

Q1 Give two reasons why animals have been domesticated.

Q2 Why might cattle be selectively bred?

Q3 Give one example of how farming practices can reduce biodiversity.

Exam Question

Q1 Archaeological excavation of an 11 000-year-old farming settlement in Syria has uncovered preserved rye seeds that show several differences to wild rye seeds found in nearby areas.

a) Explain how selective breeding could account for the differences between the wild rye seeds and the seeds from the settlement. [2 marks]

b) Suggest two characteristics that may have been selected for in the rye. [2 marks]

c) Explain why early farming settlements like this were able to support a larger population than hunter-gatherer societies. [2 marks]

Disgruntled wives grew crops in the hopes of getting a larger settlement...

So, there you go. Over the past 12 000 years or so we've made some pretty drastic changes to the environment, often in the name of farming. It hasn't stopped though — we're still at it, chopping down the rainforest so there's more land to grow things like coffee beans and to graze cattle so the world's supplied with juicy burgers... mmmm... coffee and burgers...

How to Interpret Experiment and Study Data

Science is all about getting good evidence to test your theories... so scientists need to be able to spot a badly designed experiment or study a mile off, and be able to interpret the results of an experiment or study properly. Being the cheeky little monkeys they are, your exam board will want to make sure you can do it too. Here's a quick reference section to show you how to go about interpreting data-style questions.

Here Are Some **Things** You Might be **Asked** to do...

For other examples check the interpreting data pages in the sections.

Here are two examples of the kind of data you could expect to get:

Experiment A

Experiment A examined the effect of temperature on the rate of an enzyme-controlled reaction. The rate of reaction for enzyme X was measured at six different temperatures (from 10 to 60 °C). All other variables were kept constant. A negative control containing all solutions except the enzyme was included. The rate of reaction for the negative control was zero at each temperature used. The results are shown in the graph below.

The effect of temperature on the rate of an enzyme-controlled reaction

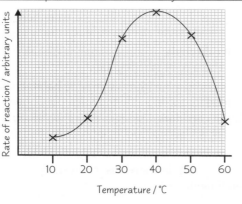

Study B

Study B examined the effect of farm hedgerow length on the number of species in a given area. The number of species present during a single week on 12 farms was counted by placing ground-level traps. All the farms were a similar area. The traps were left out every day, at 6 am for two hours and once again at 6 pm for two hours. The data was plotted against hedgerow length. The results are shown in the scattergram below.

The effect of hedgerow length on number of species

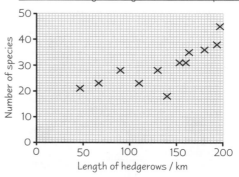

1) Describe the Data

You need to be able to **describe** any data you're given. The level of **detail** in your answer should be appropriate for the **number of marks** given. Loads of marks = more detail, few marks = less detail.
For the two examples above:

Example — Experiment A

1) The data shows that the **rate of reaction increases** as **temperature increases** up to a **certain point**. The rate of reaction then **decreases** as temperature increases (2 marks).

2) The data shows that the rate of reaction **increases** as temperature increases from **10 °C** up to **40 °C**. The rate of reaction then **decreases** as temperature increases from **40 °C to 60 °C** (4 marks).

Example — Study B

The data shows a **positive correlation** between the length of hedgerows and the number of species in the area (1 mark).

Correlation describes the **relationship** between two variables — the one that's been changed and the one that's been measured. Data can show **three** types of correlation:

1) **Positive** — as one variable **increases** the other **increases**.

2) **Negative** — as one variable **increases** the other **decreases**.

3) **None** — there is **no relationship** between the two variables.

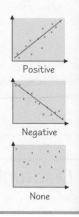

How to Interpret Experiment and Study Data

2) Draw or Check the Conclusions

1) Ideally, only **two** quantities would ever change in any experiment or study — everything else would be **constant**.

2) If you can keep everything else constant and the results show a correlation then you **can** conclude that the change in one variable **does cause** the change in the other. ➡

3) But usually all the variables **can't** be controlled, so other **factors** (that you **couldn't** keep constant) could be having an **effect**.

4) Because of this, scientists have to be very careful when **drawing conclusions**. Most results show a **link** (correlation) between the variables, but that **doesn't prove that a change in one causes the change in the other**. ➡

5) The **data** should always **support** the conclusion. This may sound obvious but it's easy to **jump** to conclusions. Conclusions have to be **precise** — not make sweeping generalisations. ➡

Example — Experiment A

All other variables were **kept constant**. E.g. pH, enzyme concentration and substrate concentration **stayed the same** each time, so these **couldn't** have influenced the change in the rate of reaction. So you **can say** that an increase in temperature **causes** an increase in the rate of reaction up to a certain point.

Example — Study B

The length of hedgerows shows a **positive correlation** with the number of species in that area. But you **can't** conclude that fewer hedgerows **causes** fewer species. **Other factors** may have been involved, e.g. the number of **predators** of the species studied may have increased in some areas, the farmers may have used **more pesticide** in one area, or something else you hadn't thought of could have caused the pattern...

Example — Experiment A

A science magazine **concluded** from this data that enzyme X works best at **40 °C**. The data **doesn't** support this. The enzyme **could** work best at 42 °C, or 47 °C but you can't tell from the data because **increases** of **10 °C** at a time were used. The rates of reaction at in-between temperatures **weren't** measured.

3) Comment on the Reliability of the Results

Reliable means the results can be **consistently reproduced** in independent experiments. And if the results are reproducible they're more likely to be **true**. If the data isn't reliable for whatever reason you **can't draw** a valid **conclusion**. Here are some of the things that affect the reliability of data:

1) <u>Size of the data set</u> — For experiments, the **more repeats** you do, the **more reliable** the data. If you get the **same result** twice, it could be the correct answer. But if you get the same result **20 times**, it's much more reliable. The general rule for **studies** is the **larger** the sample size, the more **reliable** the **data** is.

Davina wasn't sure she'd got a large enough sample size.

E.g. Study B is quite **small** — they only used 12 farms. The **trend** shown by the data may not appear if you studied **50 or 100 farms**, or studied them for a longer period of time.

2) <u>Variables</u> — The **more variables** you **control**, the **more reliable** your data is. In an experiment you would control all the variables, but when doing a study this isn't always possible. You try to control **as many as possible** or use **matched groups** (see page 3).

E.g. ideally, all the farms in Study B would have a similar **type** of land, similar **weather**, have the same **crops** growing, etc. Then you could be more sure that the one factor being **investigated** (hedgerows) is having an **effect** on the thing being **measured** (number of species). In Experiment A, **all** other variables were controlled, e.g. pH, concentrations, volumes, so you can be sure the temperature is causing the **change** in the **reaction rate**.

Jane rarely ate chocolate, honestly.

3) <u>Data collection</u> — think about all the **problems** with the **method** and see if **bias** has slipped in. For example, members of the public sometimes tell **little porkies**, so it's easy for studies involving **questionnaires** to be **biased**. E.g. people often underestimate how much alcohol they drink or how many cigarettes they smoke.

E.g. in Study B, the traps were placed on the **ground**, so species like birds weren't included. The traps weren't left overnight, so **nocturnal** animals wouldn't get counted, etc. This could have affected the results.

How to Interpret Experiment and Study Data

4) <u>Controls</u> — without controls, it's very difficult to **draw valid conclusions**. **Negative controls** are used to make sure that nothing you're doing in the experiment has an effect, **other than** what you're testing. But it's not always possible to have controls in studies (study controls usually involve a group where **nothing changes**, e.g. a group of patients aren't given a new long-term treatment to make sure any effects detected in the patients having the treatment aren't due to the fact that they've had two months to recover).

E.g. in Experiment A, the **negative control** contained everything from the experiment **except** the enzyme. This was used to show that the change in reaction rate was caused by the effect of **temperature** on the **enzyme**, and nothing else. If something else in the experiment (e.g. the water, or something in the test tube) was causing the change, you would get the **same results** in the negative control (and you'd know something was up).

5) <u>Repetition by other scientists</u> — for theories to become accepted as 'fact' other scientists need to **repeat** the work (see page 2). If **multiple studies** or **experiments** come to the same conclusion, then that conclusion is **more reliable**.

E.g. if a second group of scientists carried out the same experiment for enzyme X and got the same results, the results would be **more reliable**.

4) Analyse the Data

Sometimes it's easier to **compare data** by making a few calculations first, e.g. converting raw data into **ratios** or **percentages**.

| Example | Three UK hospitals have been trying out three **different methods** to **control the spread** of chest infections. A study investigated the number of people suffering from chest infections in those hospitals over a **three month period**. The table opposite shows the results. If you just look at the **number of cases** in the **last month** (March) then the method of hospital 3 appears to have worked **least well**, as they have the **highest number** of infections. But if you look at the **percentage increase** in infections you get a different picture: hospital 1 = 30%, hospital 2 = 293%, and hospital 3 = 18%. So hospital 3 has the lowest percentage increase, suggesting their method of control is **working the best**.

	Number of cases per 6000 patients		
Hospital	Jan	Feb	March
1	60	65	78
2	14	24	55
3	93	96	110

Calculating percentage increase, hospital 1:

$$\frac{(78 - 60)}{60} \times 100 = \frac{18}{60} \times 100 = 30\%$$

There Are a Few Technical Terms You Need to Understand

I'm sure you probably know these all off by heart, but it's easy to get mixed up sometimes. So here's a quick recap of some words **commonly used** when assessing and analysing experiments and studies:

1) **Variable** — A variable is a **quantity** that has the **potential to change**, e.g. weight. There are two types of variable commonly referred to in experiments:

- **Independent variable** — the thing that's **changed** in an experiment.
- **Dependent variable** — the thing that you **measure** in an experiment.

When drawing graphs, the dependent variable should go on the y-axis (the vertical axis) and the independent on the x-axis (the horizontal axis).

2) **Accurate** — Accurate results are those that are **really close** to the **true** answer.

3) **Precise results** — These are results taken using **sensitive instruments** that measure in **small increments**, e.g. pH measured with a meter (pH 7.692) will be **more precise** than pH measured with paper (pH 8).

*It's possible for results to be precise **but not** accurate, e.g. a balance that weighs to 1/1000 th of a gram will give precise results, but if it's not **calibrated** properly the results won't be accurate.*

4) **Qualitative** — A **qualitative** test tells you **what's** present, e.g. an acid or an alkali.

5) **Quantitative** — A **quantitative** test tells you **how much** is present, e.g. an acid that's pH 2.46.

Controls — I think I prefer the remote kind...

*These pages should give you a fair idea of the points to think about when interpreting data. Just use your head and remember the three main points in the checklist — **d**escribe the **d**ata, **c**heck the **c**onclusions and make sure the **r**esults are **r**eliable.*

Answers

Unit 1: Section 1 — Diet
Page 5 — Balanced Diet

1 a) Maximum of 5 marks available.
Carbohydrates provide energy *[1 mark]*. Fats act as an energy store / provide insulation / make up cell membranes / physically protect cells *[1 mark]*. Protein is needed for growth / repair of tissue / making enzymes *[1 mark]*. Fibre keeps the gut in good working order *[1 mark]*. Water is used in chemical reactions *[1 mark]*.

b) Maximum of 4 marks available.
Fruits and vegetables are good sources of vitamins, minerals and fibre *[1 mark]*. Studies have shown they can reduce the risk of heart disease and certain cancers *[1 mark]*. Eating too much salt can cause high blood pressure *[1 mark]*. Eating too much fat can lead to weight gain and conditions like obesity and heart disease *[1 mark]*.

Page 7 — Diet and Disease

1 a) Maximum of 2 marks available.
The incidence of cancer increases with age *[1 mark]*. After the age of 30, the more alcohol consumed per day, the higher the incidence of cancer *[1 mark]*.

b) Maximum of 2 marks available.
No, a correlation does not mean that one factor directly causes another *[1 mark]*. There could be other factors, e.g. another chemical in the alcoholic drink may be causing the cancer etc. *[1 mark]*.

c) Maximum of 1 mark available.
Evaluation by other experts in the same field to assess the quality of a piece work *[1 mark]*.

Page 9 — Evaluating the Nutritional Value of Food

1 a) Maximum of 6 marks available
Both pizzas have a high level of fat *[1 mark]*, saturated fat *[1 mark]*, and salt *[1 mark]*. Pizza A has a lower amount of sugar than pizza B *[1 mark]*, and fewer calories *[1 mark]*. Both pizzas are quite unhealthy, but on the whole pizza A is slightly less unhealthy *[1 mark]*.

b) Maximum of 1 mark available
Eating too much of this product could lead to weight gain/ high blood pressure/other suitable example *[1 mark]*.

c) Maximum of 2 marks available.
Protein content *[1 mark]* and fibre content *[1 mark]*.

Page 11 — Composition of Food

1 Maximum of 10 marks available.
Proteins are made from amino acids *[1 mark]*. The amino acids are joined together in a long (polypeptide) chain *[1 mark]*. The sequence of amino acids is the protein's primary structure *[1 mark]*. The amino acid chain/polypeptide coils or folds in a certain way *[1 mark]*. The way it's coiled or folded is the protein's secondary structure *[1 mark]*. The coiled or folded chain is itself folded into a specific 3D shape *[1 mark]*. This is the protein's tertiary structure *[1 mark]*. The tertiary structure is held together by hydrogen bonds *[1 mark]*, ionic bonds *[1 mark]* and disulphide bridges *[1 mark]*.

Page 13 — Digestion of Food and Chromatography

1 a) Maximum of 6 marks available, one for each filled-in box.

Enzyme	Hydrolyses:	Products of hydrolysis:	Conditions required:	Location of reaction:
pepsin	protein	amino acids /smaller peptides	acidic	stomach
lipase	fat	fatty acids and glycerol	alkaline	small intestine
carbohydrase	carbohydrate	monosaccharides	alkaline	small intestine

b) Maximum of 2 marks available.
The stomach produces acid which lowers pH/makes it more acidic *[1 mark]* and the liver produces bile which raises pH/ makes it more alkaline *[1 mark]*.

c) Maximum of 3 marks available.
During hydrolysis, the bonds between monomers in a polymer are broken *[1 mark]* by adding water *[1 mark]*. Hydrolysis is important because it breaks large, insoluble molecules into smaller, soluble molecules so they can be absorbed by the body *[1 mark]*.

Unit 1: Section 2 — Enzymes
Page 15 — Action of Enzymes

1 Maximum of 7 marks available.
In the 'lock and key' model the enzyme and the substrate have to fit together at the active site of the enzyme *[1 mark]*. This creates an enzyme-substrate complex *[1 mark]*. The active site then causes changes in the substrate *[1 mark]*. This mark could also be gained by explaining the change (e.g. bringing molecules closer together, or putting a strain on bonds). The change results in the substrate being broken down/joined together *[1 mark]*.
The 'induced fit' model has the same basic mechanism as the 'lock and key' model *[1 mark]*.
The difference is that the substrate is thought to cause a change in the enzyme's active site shape *[1 mark]*, which enables a better fit *[1 mark]*.

Page 17 — Enzyme Activity and Digestive Enzymes

1 Maximum of 8 marks available, from any of the 10 points below.
If the solution is too cold, the enzyme will work very slowly *[1 mark]*. This is because, at low temperatures, the molecules have little kinetic energy, so move slowly, making collisions between enzyme and substrate molecules less likely *[1 mark]*. Also, fewer of the collisions will have enough energy to result in a reaction *[1 mark]*.
The marks above could also be obtained by giving the reverse argument — a higher temperature is best to use because the molecules will move fast enough to give a reasonable chance of collisions and those collisions will have more energy, so more will result in a reaction.
If the temperature gets too high, the reaction will stop *[1 mark]*. This is because the enzyme is denatured *[1 mark]* — the active site changes shape and will no longer fit the substrate *[1 mark]*. Denaturation is caused by increased vibration breaking bonds in the enzyme *[1 mark]*. Enzymes have an optimum pH *[1 mark]*. pH values too far from the optimum cause denaturation *[1 mark]*.
Explanation of denaturation here will get a mark only if it hasn't been explained earlier.
Denaturation by pH is caused by disruption of ionic and hydrogen bonds, which alters the enzyme's tertiary structure *[1 mark]*.

Answers

2   Maximum of 2 marks available.
     The sweetener molecules will be a different shape to natural sugars [1 mark] so won't fit into the active site of any of our digestive enzymes [1 mark].

Page 19 — Enzymes in Medicine

1 a) Maximum of 4 marks available.
     Glucose oxidase catalyses the reaction between glucose, oxygen and water [1 mark]. If glucose is present in a sample, hydrogen peroxide is produced [1 mark]. Hydrogen peroxide reacts with a dye in the reagent strip, causing a colour change [1 mark]. This reaction is catalysed by peroxidase [1 mark].
  b) Maximum of 2 marks available.
     The enzyme glucose oxidase is specific to glucose, because only glucose has the right shaped molecule [1 mark] to fit its active site [1 mark].

2   Maximum of 3 marks available.
     Elastase breaks down elastin in old or damaged tissue, and also has the potential to break down elastin in healthy lung tissue [1 mark]. Alpha-1-antitrypsin normally inhibits elastase, preventing break down of healthy tissue [1 mark]. In alpha-1-antitrypsin deficiency, the elastase isn't inhibited and elastin in lung tissue is broken down, which leads to emphysema [1 mark].

3   Maximum of 3 marks available.
     Pancreatitis reduces the ability of the pancreas to produce enzymes [1 mark]. This results in changes in the concentration and distribution of enzymes in the gut [1 mark]. This could be treated by taking pain-relieving drugs / by eating a specially designed diet [1 mark].

Unit 1: Section 3 — Cystic Fibrosis
Page 21 — Gas Exchange

1   Maximum of 6 marks available.
     The lungs have a large surface area [1 mark] because of the large number of alveoli they contain [1 mark]. The alveolar epithelium and capillary endothelium are each only one layer of cells thick [1 mark], which decreases the distance gases have to diffuse across [1 mark]. There is a large concentration gradient of respiratory gases between the alveoli and blood capillaries [1 mark], maintained by ventilation [1 mark].
     This question asks you to 'explain'. So you won't get full marks by just writing down the three factors that make lungs efficient at gas exchange. You need to ask yourself 'why do lungs have a large surface area, a short diffusion pathway and a large concentration gradient?'

2   Maximum of 4 marks available.
     Thick mucus builds up and narrows the airways [1 mark], so a lower volume of air is taken in, which decreases the concentration gradient between the lungs and the blood [1 mark]. Thick mucus may form a mucus plug, completely blocking an airway [1 mark] so a number of alveoli cannot carry out gas exchange [1 mark].

Page 23 — Mucus Production

1   Maximum of 8 marks available.
     The defective CFTR protein is unable to transport/pump chloride ions out of the cell [1 mark]. Chloride ions are trapped inside the cell [1 mark]. This lowers the water potential inside the cell [1 mark]. The water potential inside the cell is lower than outside the cell [1 mark]. Water does not move out of the cell and into the mucus by osmosis [1 mark]. The mucus becomes dehydrated and sticky [1 mark]. Ciliated cells can no longer move the mucus upwards [1 mark] so the mucus accumulates and becomes thicker [1 mark].

2   Maximum of 4 marks available.
     Mucus in the lungs traps bacteria [1 mark] and is then coughed up or swallowed and destroyed [1 mark]. People suffering from cystic fibrosis can't clear the mucus from their lungs [1 mark]. Bacteria multiply in their lungs, causing infections [1 mark].

Page 25 — Mucus Production

1   Maximum of 6 marks available.
     The CFTR protein is made at the ribosomes [1 mark]. The protein is folded and processed at the rough endoplasmic reticulum [1 mark]. The protein is transported to the Golgi body in vesicles [1 mark]. At the Golgi body the CFTR protein undergoes further processing [1 mark]. The CFTR protein is transported to the plasma membrane in vesicles [1 mark], where it is inserted into the membrane [1 mark].
     This question asks how the CFTR protein is produced, so remember that it is inserted into the plasma membrane, whereas the proteins in mucus (glycoproteins) are secreted from the cell.

2 a) Maximum of 2 marks available.
     Mucus prevents enzymes being released [1 mark]. Nutrients can't be absorbed from undigested food [1 mark].
  b) Maximum of 2 marks available.
     Mucus blocks the pancreatic duct [1 mark]. Pancreatic enzymes digest the pancreas [1 mark].

Unit 1: Section 4 — Microorganisms and Disease
Page 27 — Bacteria

1   Maximum of 3 marks available, from any of the 4 points below.
     Tuberculosis is caused by a bacterium called Mycobacterium tuberculosis [1 mark]. Symptoms include weight loss and coughing [1 mark]. TB can be controlled using the BCG vaccine to prevent infection [1 mark] and antibiotics to get rid of infection [1 mark].
     As the question asks for cause, symptoms and control and the question is worth 3 marks you should include a point on each.

2   Maximum of 4 marks available.
     Ribosomes are the site of protein synthesis [1 mark]. If the ribosomes are inhibited, proteins can't be made [1 mark]. Enzymes are proteins, so inhibiting ribosomes also means that enzymes can't be made [1 mark] and so the cell can't carry out its metabolic processes [1 mark].

Answers

Page 29 — Evaluating Resistance Data

1 a) Maximum of 2 marks available.
The number of death certificates mentioning S. aureus stayed roughly the same *[1 mark]*. The number of death certificates mentioning MRSA increased *[1 mark]*.

b) Maximum of 2 marks available, from any of the 3 points below.
The time period is quite short, so this may not be the general trend *[1 mark]*. The death certificates only mentioned MRSA or S. aureus, so they might not actually be causing the deaths *[1 mark]*. The increased publicity surrounding MRSA may influence the decisions to include it on the death certificate, which could affect the results *[1 mark]*.

Page 31 — Viruses

1 Maximum of 5 marks available.
HIV has a core that contains the genetic material (RNA) *[1 mark]* and some proteins *[1 mark]*. It has an outer layer called the capsid, which is made of protein *[1 mark]*, surrounded by an envelope that is made from the membrane of the host cell *[1 mark]*.
A final mark is available for providing a diagram *[1 mark]*.

Capsid   Envelope
Genetic material

2 Maximum of 4 marks available.
An integrase inhibitor would prevent HIV from integrating its genetic material into the host's DNA *[1 mark]*. So HIV couldn't replicate *[1 mark]*. The host cell doesn't use integrase *[1 mark]* so wouldn't be affected *[1 mark]*.

Unit 1: Section 5 — The Immune System
Page 33 — The Immune Response

1 Maximum of 10 marks available.
When Emily caught chickenpox the first time *[1 mark]* her B- and T-cells produced memory cells *[1 mark]* giving her immunological memory against the virus antigens *[1 mark]*. When exposed a second time *[1 mark]* the memory B-cells divided into plasma cells *[1 mark]* to produce the right antibody to the virus *[1 mark]*. The memory T-cells divided into the correct type of T-cell *[1 mark]* to kill the virus *[1 mark]*. The secondary response was quicker and stronger *[1 mark]* and so got rid of the pathogen before she showed any symptoms *[1 mark]*.
This question is asking about the secondary response and the immune system memory, so no detail is needed about how the primary response got rid of the infection.

2 Maximum of 3 marks available.
Antibodies coat pathogens, making it easier for phagocytes to engulf them *[1 mark]* and preventing them from entering host cells *[1 mark]*. They also bind to toxins to neutralise them *[1 mark]*.
There are three marks available for this question, so you need to think of three different functions.

Page 35 — Vaccines

1 Maximum of 5 marks available.
a) Because people were immunised against Hib *[1 mark]* and also had the protection of herd immunity *[1 mark]*.

b) The number of cases of Hib increased *[1 mark]*.
c) Dead microorganism *[1 mark]*, attenuated microorganism *[1 mark]*.

Page 37 — Antibodies in Medicine

1 Maximum of 4 marks available.
A pregnancy test contains antibodies that only bind to hCG *[1 mark]*. Antibodies are proteins that have specific tertiary structures *[1 mark]*. This gives them specific binding sites *[1 mark]* that only molecules with a complementary shape will fit into *[1 mark]*.

2 Maximum of 4 marks available.
Monoclonal antibodies are made against antigens specific to cancer cells *[1 mark]*. An anti-cancer drug is attached to the antibodies *[1 mark]*. The antibodies bind to tumour markers on cancer cells because their binding sites have a complementary shape *[1 mark]*. This delivers the anti-cancer drug to the cells *[1 mark]*.

Unit 1: Section 6 — Cardiovascular Disease
Page 39 — The Heart

1 Maximum of 3 marks available, from any of the 4 points below.
Pressure increases in the atria when they contract and in the ventricles when they contract *[1 mark]*. The pressure in the ventricles also increases as they receive the ejected blood from the atria *[1 mark]*. Pressure decreases in the atria when they relax and in the ventricles when they relax *[1 mark]*. There's more pressure during contraction in the left ventricle than the right ventricle, because of the thicker muscle walls producing more force *[1 mark]*.
This question doesn't ask you to describe the cardiac cycle — it specifically asks you to describe the pressure changes during contraction and relaxation. Make sure you mention both atria and ventricles in your answer.

2 Maximum of 6 marks available.
The valves only open one way *[1 mark]*.
Whether they open or close depends on the relative pressure of the heart chambers *[1 mark]*. If the pressure is greater behind a valve (i.e. there's lots of blood in the chamber behind it) *[1 mark]*, it's forced open, to let the blood travel in the right direction *[1 mark]*. Once the blood's gone through the valve, the pressure is greater in front of the valve *[1 mark]*, which forces it shut, preventing blood from flowing back into the chamber *[1 mark]*.
Here you need to explain how valves function in relation to blood flow, rather than just in relation to relative pressures.

Page 41 — Blood Vessels

1 Maximum of 4 marks available.
At the start of the capillary bed, the pressure in the capillaries is greater than the pressure in the tissue fluid outside the capillaries *[1 mark]*. This means fluid from the blood is forced out of the capillaries *[1 mark]*. Fluid loss causes the water potential of blood capillaries to become lower than that of tissue fluid *[1 mark]*. So fluid moves back into the capillaries at the vein end of the capillary bed by osmosis *[1 mark]*.

Answers

2   *Maximum of 2 marks available.*
Their walls are only one cell thick to allow efficient diffusion of substances (e.g. glucose and oxygen) [1 mark]. Capillaries form networks called capillary beds, which provide a large surface area for exchange [1 mark].

Page 43 — Cardiovascular Disease

1   *Maximum of 2 marks available.*
An atheroma plaque may break through the inner lining of the artery, leaving a rough surface [1 mark]. This damage causes a blood clot (thrombus) to form over the area [1 mark].
This question is not asking about the consequences of thrombosis, so no extra marks will be given if you write about it.

2   *Maximum of 4 marks available.*
Atheroma formation narrows the coronary arteries [1 mark], which reduces the flow of blood to the heart [1 mark]. This reduces the supply of oxygen to the heart muscle [1 mark] which causes chest pain [1 mark].

Page 45 — Lifestyle and Cardiovascular Disease

1 a) *Maximum of 2 marks available.*
A large sample size was used [1 mark]. The sample included many countries [1 mark].
 b) *Maximum of 2 marks available.*
Other risk factors must have been identified [1 mark], and groups with similar risk factors compared [1 mark].
 c) *Maximum of 2 marks available.*
A large waist measurement indicates that someone is overweight/obese [1 mark], which may increase their blood pressure and blood cholesterol levels [1 mark].

Unit 2: Section 1 — Genetics
Page 47 — DNA — The Basics

1   *Maximum of 4 marks available, from any of the 5 points below.*
Nucleotides are joined between the phosphate group of one nucleotide and the sugar of the next [1 mark] forming the sugar-phosphate backbone [1 mark]. The two polynucleotide strands join through hydrogen bonds [1 mark] between the base pairs [1 mark].
The final mark is given for at least one accurate diagram showing at least one of the above points [1 mark].
As the question asks for a diagram make sure you do at least one, e.g.:

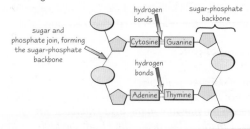

Page 49 — Protein Synthesis and DNA Replication

1   *Maximum of 4 marks available.*
The DNA sequence codes for the sequence of amino acids in proteins [1 mark]. Enzymes are proteins, so DNA codes for all enzymes [1 mark]. Enzymes control metabolic pathways [1 mark]. Metabolic pathways help to determine phenotype (physical appearance) [1 mark].

2   *Maximum of 7 marks available.*
The DNA helix unzips [1 mark]. Each strand acts as a template [1 mark]. Individual free DNA nucleotides join up along the template strand by specific base pairing [1 mark]. DNA polymerase joins the individual nucleotides together [1 mark].
(Students often forget to mention this enzyme in their answers — make sure you don't forget.)
Hydrogen bonds then form between the bases on each strand [1 mark]. Two identical DNA molecules are produced [1 mark]. Each of the new molecules contains a single strand from the original DNA molecule and a single new strand [1 mark].

Unit 2: Section 2 — Cell Division and Cancer
Page 51 — The Cell Cycle and Mitosis

1 a) *Maximum of 6 marks available.*
A = Metaphase [1 mark], because the chromosomes are lined up at the middle of the cell [1 mark].
B = Telophase [1 mark], because there are now two nuclei and the cytoplasm is dividing to form two new cells [1 mark].
C = Anaphase [1 mark], because the centromeres have divided and the chromatids are moving to opposite ends of the cell [1 mark].
If you've learned the diagrams of what happens at each stage of mitosis, this should be a breeze. That's why it'd be a total disaster if you lost three marks for forgetting to give reasons for your answers. Always read the question properly and do exactly what it tells you to do.
 b) *Maximum of 3 marks available:*
X = Chromatid [1 mark].
Y = Centromere [1 mark].
Z = Spindle fibre [1 mark].

Page 53 — Cancer

1 a) *Maximum of 2 marks available, from any of the 3 points below.*
Malignant tumours are cancers. Benign tumours are not cancerous [1 mark]. Malignant tumours usually grow rapidly, invading and destroying surrounding tissues. Benign tumours usually grow slower than malignant tumours [1 mark]. Malignant tumours can spread, benign tumours can't [1 mark].
 b) *Maximum of 5 marks available.*
Cells break off the primary tumour in the breast [1 mark]. The cells enter the bloodstream (or lymphatic system) [1 mark]. The cancer cells continue to divide in the bloodstream (or lymphatic system) [1 mark]. Cells invade the ulna [1 mark] and form a secondary tumour [1 mark].
 c) *Maximum of 5 marks available.*
If a mutation occurs in a tumour suppressor gene [1 mark], proteins that stop cells dividing and cause cell death might not be produced [1 mark]. This allows cells to grow and divide uncontrollably [1 mark]. If a mutation occurs in a growth promotion gene [1 mark], the gene can become 'hyperactive', causing the cell to grow and divide uncontrollably [1 mark].

Answers

2   Maximum of 4 marks available, from any of the 8 points below.
     Tumour cells can have an irregular shape *[1 mark]*.
     The nucleus of tumour cells can be larger *[1 mark]* and
     darker *[1 mark]* than normal cells. Sometimes tumour cells
     have more than one nucleus *[1 mark]*. Tumour cells don't
     produce all the proteins needed to function correctly
     [1 mark]. Tumour cells have different antigens on their
     surface *[1 mark]*. Tumour cells don't respond to growth
     regulating processes *[1 mark]*. Tumour cells divide
     (by mitosis) more frequently than normal cells *[1 mark]*.

Page 55 — Interpreting Cancer Data

1 a) Maximum of 1 mark.
      There is a positive correlation between the number of times
      a person has been severely sunburnt and the relative risk of
      malignant melanoma *[1 mark]*.
  b) Maximum of 1 mark.
      To increase the reliability / accuracy of results *[1 mark]*.
  c) Maximum of 2 marks.
      Sunburn is caused by high levels of exposure to the
      ultraviolet radiation in sunlight *[1 mark]*. UV radiation can
      cause mutations in genes, which can lead to cancer
      [1 mark].

Page 57 — Meiosis

1   Maximum of 2 marks available.
     Normal body cells have two copies of each chromosome
     [1 mark]. Gametes have to have half the number of
     chromosomes so that when fertilisation takes place,
     the resulting embryo will have the correct diploid number
     [1 mark].

2   Maximum of 3 marks available.
     A = 23 *[1 mark]*, B = 23 *[1 mark]*, C = 46 (23 pairs) *[1 mark]*.

3 a) Maximum of 3 marks available.
      Chromosome 21 fails to separate properly during meiosis
      [1 mark]. So, one gamete will end up with two chromosome
      21's *[1 mark]*. If this gamete fuses with another gamete at
      fertilisation the zygote will contain 3 copies of chromosome
      21 *[1 mark]*.
  b) Maximum of 1 mark available.
      Non-disjunction *[1 mark]*.

Unit 2: Section 3 — Evolution of Humans
Page 59 — Classification

1   Maximum of 7 marks available.

Kingdom	Phylum	Class	Order	Family	Genus	Species
Animalia	Chordata	Mammalia	Primates	Hominidae	Homo	sapiens

[1 mark for each correct answer]

2   Maximum of 2 marks available, from any of the 5 points below.
     Biochemical *[1 mark]*, anatomical *[1 mark]*, embryological
     [1 mark], immunological *[1 mark]*, behavioural *[1 mark]*.

Page 61 — Evolution

1 a) i) Maximum of 2 marks available.
         During its lifetime, the bat stretches and lengthens its
         tongue whilst reaching for the nectar *[1 mark]*.
         The longer tongues are passed on to offspring *[1 mark]*.
      ii) Maximum of 1 mark available.
         Acquired characteristics are not passed on to the next
         generation *[1 mark]*.
  b) Maximum of 3 marks available.
      There will be variation in tongue length within a population of
      bats *[1 mark]*. Bats with longer tongues will be able to feed
      from the flowers and so will be more likely to survive to
      reproduce *[1 mark]*. The alleles for longer tongues are more
      likely to be passed on to the next generation *[1 mark]*.

Page 63 — Evidence for Evolution

1 a) Maximum of 2 marks available, 1 mark for noting the
      development of fingers (finger-like appendages) and 1 mark
      for any of the explanations as to why.
      E.g. as the snozcumber moved from grazing to living in the
      forests the hands evolved to have fingers *[1 mark]* to enable
      the manipulation of tools *[1 mark]* / to allow food to be
      picked *[1 mark]* / to grip branches in the forest *[1 mark]*.
  b) Maximum of 2 marks available, from any of the 3 points below.
      There are only three fossils covering a long time period
      [1 mark]. There's a large time gap in the record (2 million to
      100 000 years ago) with no fossils *[1 mark]*. There are no
      in-between fossils showing the change from a 'stump' to five
      fingers *[1 mark]*.

Page 65 — Speciation

1 a) Maximum of 1 mark available.
      The new species could not interbreed with each other
      [1 mark].
  b) Maximum of 3 marks available.
      Different populations of flies were isolated and fed on
      different foods *[1 mark]*. This caused changes in allele
      frequencies between the populations *[1 mark]*, which made
      them reproductively isolated and eventually resulted in
      speciation *[1 mark]*.
  c) Maximum of 2 marks available, from any of the 3 points below.
      Seasonal changes (become sexually active at different times)
      [1 mark]. Mechanical changes (changes to genitalia)
      [1 mark]. Behavioural changes (changes in behaviour that
      prevent mating) *[1 mark]*.
  d) Maximum of 1 mark available, from any of the 5 points below
      or any other good point.
      E.g. geographical barrier *[1 mark]*, flood *[1 mark]*, volcanic
      eruption *[1 mark]*, earthquake *[1 mark]*, glacier *[1 mark]*.
  e) Maximum of 1 mark available.
      Speciation increases the diversity of life *[1 mark]*.

Page 67 — Other Hominids

1 a) Maximum of 2 marks available, from any of the 3 points
      below or any other good point.
      E.g. examine size and shape of teeth *[1 mark]*, teeth wear
      patterns *[1 mark]*, chemical composition of bones *[1 mark]*.
  b) Maximum of 2 marks available.
      Lack of fossils (gaps) *[1 mark]*, incomplete fossils *[1 mark]*.

Answers

Page 69 — Cultural Evolution and Hunter-Gatherers

1 a) *Maximum of 2 marks available.*
   Removing meat from bones / breaking open bones [1 mark],
   because the tools were found with bone fragments [1 mark].
  b) *Maximum of 7 marks available.*
   Hunter-gatherers hunted wild animals [1 mark] and collected
   wild plants [1 mark]. They lived in small groups [1 mark]
   made up of one or more families [1 mark]. They hunted in a
   range around a home base [1 mark]. They cooperated as a
   group [1 mark]. They divided labour between all the
   members of the community [1 mark].

Unit 2: Section 4 — Adaptations to Survive
Page 71 — Anatomical and Behavioural Adaptations

1 a) *Maximum of 1 mark available.*
   Walking on two feet [1 mark].
  b) *Maximum of 2 marks available.*
   It allows us to see over obstacles, which is useful when
   finding food/spotting predators [1 mark]. The hands are freed
   up for other uses, e.g. using tools [1 mark].
  c) *Maximum of 2 marks available.*
   Opposable thumbs allow us to use tools to build shelters to
   protect us from predators and harsh weather / to hunt, which
   increases the chances of getting food [1 marks]. Paler skin
   colour helps us to synthesise vitamin D in order to survive in
   less sunny places [1 marks].

Page 73 — Physiological Adaptations

1 a) *Maximum of 5 marks available.*
   The breathing rate would go up [1 mark], because carbonic
   acid lowers blood pH [1 mark]. This stimulates
   chemoreceptors in the medulla, aortic bodies and carotid
   bodies [1 mark]. The chemoreceptors send a signal to the
   medulla [1 mark]. In turn, the medulla sends more frequent
   nerve impulses to the intercostal muscles and diaphragm
   [1 mark].
   This question only asks about the breathing rate, so you won't
   get any extra marks for commenting on the depth of breathing or
   speed of gas exchange.
  b) *Maximum of 1 mark available.*
   cardiac output (cm³/min) = heart rate (beats per minute)
   × stroke volume (cm³) [1 mark].

Page 75 — Physiological Adaptations

1 a) *Maximum of 1 mark available.*
   Anaerobic respiration [1 mark].
  b) *Maximum of 2 marks available.*
   Advantage: respiration can continue even when there is not
   enough oxygen available [1 mark]. Disadvantage: it's less
   efficient at releasing energy than aerobic respiration / lactate
   is produced, which is toxic / blood pH is lowered, which
   causes muscle fatigue [1 mark].
  c) *Maximum of 2 marks available.*
   It will decrease [1 mark], as oxygen is used to break down the
   lactate / as the lactate is converted to glucose/glycogen
   [1 mark].

Page 77 — Parasite Adaptations

1 a) *Maximum of 1 mark available.*
   (A sucker) for attachment to the gut wall [1 mark].
  b) *Maximum of 1 mark available.*
   It obtains digested food from the host [1 mark].
  c) *Maximum of 2 marks available.*
   It may produce lots of offspring [1 mark]. Many of its
   offspring will die, so producing more increases the chance of
   some offspring successfully infecting a host [1 mark].

Unit 2: Section 5 — Changing Our Environment
Page 79 — Impact of Farming on the Landscape

1. a) *Maximum of 2 marks available, from any of the 3 points below.*
   Remains of enclosed pens [1 mark]. Remains/bones of pigs
   [1 mark]. Artwork of pigs being farmed [1 mark].
   Writing that refers to pig farming [1 mark].
  b) *Maximum of 3 marks available, from any of the following.*
   Loss of woodland/deforestation [1 mark]. Increased arable or
   grazing land [1 mark]. Reduced biodiversity [1 mark].
   Changes to local weather systems, e.g. rainfall and humidity
   reduced due to deforestation [1 mark]. Increased soil erosion
   [1 mark]. Reduced soil quality [1 mark]. Increased
   heathland [1 mark].
  c) *Maximum of 2 marks available.*
   Farming caused a change in vegetation [1 mark] that resulted
   in some species dying out or leaving the area due to lack of
   food/habitats [1 mark].

Page 81 — Farming Practices and Impact on Biodiversity

1 a) *Maximum of 2 marks available.*
   Early farmers selected and cultivated rye seeds/plants with
   useful characteristics [1 mark]. Over generations this led to
   changes in the population [1 mark].
  b) *Maximum of 2 marks available, from any of the following.*
   High yield [1 mark]. High germination rate [1 mark].
   Fast growth rate [1 mark]. Resistance to disease [1 mark].
   Resistance to frost [1 mark].
  c) *Maximum of 2 marks available.*
   Growing crops and keeping animals [1 mark] led to an
   increase in food production per unit area / a food surplus
   [1 mark].

Index

Index

Index

Index